WAY MORE THAN LUCK

Page 192 represents a continuation of this copyright page.

Library of Congress Cataloging-in-Publication Data available.

ISBN: 978-1-4521-3519-9

Manufactured in China.

Design by Anne Kenady

10 9 8 7 6 5 4 3 2

Chronicle Books LLC
680 Second Street
San Francisco, CA 94107

www.chroniclebooks.com

WAY MORE THAN LUCK

THAN

LUCK

COMMENCEMENT
SPEECHES

on

LIVING WITH BRAVERY,
EMPATHY, AND OTHER
EXISTENTIAL SKILLS

CHRONICLE BOOKS

SAN FRANCISCO

Contents

Debbie Millman

SAN JOSÉ STATE UNIVERSITY, 2013

For most of my adult life, I traveled a safe path. I remember in vivid detail the moment I began my journey: August 1983, the hot muggy summer of David Bowie's *Modern Love* and *Synchronicity* by the Police. A few months after I graduated college, I stood on the corner of Seventh Avenue and Bleeker Street in New York City, wearing pastel blue trousers, a hot pink V-neck tee shirt, and bright white Capezio oxfords. I lingered at the intersection, peering deep into my future, and contemplated the choice between the secure and the uncertain, between the creative and the logical, between the known and the unknown. I dreamed of being a successful artist, but inasmuch as I knew what I wanted, I felt compelled to consider what was reasonable in order to ensure my economic security. Even though I wanted what my best friend once referred to as the whole wide world, I thought it was prudent to compromise. I told myself it was more sensible to aspire for success that was realistically attainable, perhaps even failure-proof. It never once occurred to me that I could succeed at what I dreamed of.

As I look back on this decision nearly thirty years later, I try to soothe myself with this rationale. I grew up in an atmosphere of emotional and financial disarray, so my impulse as a young woman was to be tenaciously self-sufficient. As a result, I've lived within a fairly fixed set of possibilities. I'm not an accomplished artist; I'm a brand consultant. I don't work alone painting canvases and sculpting clay in a cold and quiet studio; I work in a bustling New York City office building to create logos for fast-food restaurants and packaging for mass-market soft drinks, salty snacks, and over-the-counter pharmaceuticals. I'm not unhappy with what has transpired in the years leading up to today. Most days I consider myself incredibly lucky that I have a fun, steady job, and a good paycheck. But I know deep in my heart that I settled. I chose security and stability over artistic and emotional freedom. And I can't help but wonder what my life would be like if I had made different decisions back on that balmy night in the West Village. I'll never know.

But I've come to a realization over the years. I am not the only person who has made this choice. Not by a long shot. I discovered these common, self-imposed restrictions are rather insidious, though they start out simple enough. We begin by worrying that we aren't good enough, that we're not smart enough or talented enough to get what we want. And then we voluntarily live in this paralyzing mental framework, rather than confront our own role in this self-fulfilling paralysis. Just the possibility of failing turns into something self-fulfilling. We begin to believe that these personal restrictions are in fact fixed limitations of the world. We go on to live our lives, all the while wondering what we can change and how we can change it. And we calculate and re-calculate when we'll be ready to do the things that we really want to do. And we dream. If only. If only. One day. Someday.

START

WITH A

BIG FAT LUMP
IN YOUR THROAT.

START WITH A PROFOUND SENSE OF WRONG,
A DEEP HOMESICKNESS, A CRAZY LOVESICKNESS,

and

RUN WITH IT.

IN ORDER
TO STRIVE FOR

A

REMARKABLE

LIFE

YOU HAVE
TO DECIDE THAT

YOU WANT ONE.

I began to rewrite the
possibilities of what comes
next. So far, the results have
surprised me. Sometimes
they scare me. Sometimes
they baffle me. Most times
I'm just glad that I'm
feeling something real.

But every once in a while, often when we least expect it, we encounter someone more courageous, someone who chose to strive for that which seemed to us unrealistically attainable, even elusive. And we marvel. We swoon. We gape. Often we are in awe. I think we look at these people as lucky, when in fact luck has nothing to do with it. It is really about the strength of their imagination. It is about how they constructed the possibilities for their life. In short: unlike me, they didn't determine what was impossible before it was possible.

John Maeda once explained the computer will do anything within its abilities, but it will do absolutely nothing unless commanded to do so. I think that people are the same. We like to operate within our abilities. But whereas the computer has a fixed code, our abilities are limited only by our perceptions. Three decades since determining my code, and after two-and-a-half decades of walking one path, I began to rewrite the possibilities of what comes next. So far, the results have surprised me. Sometimes they scare me. Sometimes they baffle me. Most times I'm just glad that I'm feeling something real.

But there hasn't been one minute during this time that I haven't wished I started sooner. I really don't know what I was waiting for. The grand scheme of a life—maybe, just maybe—is not about knowing or not knowing, choosing or not choosing. Perhaps what is truly known can't be described or articulated by creativity or logic, science or art. Perhaps it can be expressed by the most authentic and meaningful combination of the two: poetry.

As Robert Frost once wrote, "A poem begins as a lump in the throat, a sense of wrong, a homesickness, a lovesickness. It is never a thought to begin with."

I recommend the following course of action for those, like you, who are just starting out, or who, like me, may be re-configuring midway through. Heed the words of Robert Frost. Start with a big fat lump in your throat. Start with a profound sense of wrong, a deep homesickness, a crazy lovesickness, and run with it. If you imagine less, less will be what you undoubtedly deserve. Do what you love. And don't stop until you get what you love. Work as hard as you can. Imagine immensities. Don't compromise and don't waste time. In order to strive for a remarkable life, you have to decide that you want one. Start now. Not twenty years from now. Not thirty years from now. Not two weeks from now. Now.

Congratulations on this important day.

····· DEBBIE MILLMAN ·····

is a design industry leader. She is the host
of the award-winning podcast *Design Matters* and
president of the design department at Sterling
Brands. She is also a president emeritus of AIGA,
and co-founder and chair of the Masters in Branding
Program at the School of Visual Arts in New York.
Millman has authored several books on design and is
a regularly contributing editor to *Print* magazine.
She lives in New York City.

Dick Costolo

UNIVERSITY OF MICHIGAN, ANN ARBOR, 2013

You know I have to start by tweeting this . . . I'm a professional, so this will only take a second.

I'd like to take a moment to thank my mother and father, and to remind you to thank your parents or whoever helped you get where you are today. They have sacrificed greatly for you. And we'll be out of here by 3:30, I promise.

When I woke up this morning and started writing my speech I was thinking about my first month on campus when I was a freshman. The football team went into that season ranked #1 in the nation in preseason. There was all this excitement on campus leading up to our first game, which was against Wisconsin, so we went up there—and we lost 21-14. There was this crushing disappointment afterwards. And I'd like you to think of that, soaring expectations followed by crushing disappointment, as a metaphor for your next twenty minutes with me.

When I was sitting where you are so many years ago, but what seems like just yesterday, I was earning my degree in computer science [crowd cheers]. Yay, nerds. At the time the CS department was in the School of Life Science and the Arts, so I needed a certain number of arts credits in order to graduate. So first semester of senior year I thought, "I'll take an acting class because we won't have a lot of homework, and I'll just go in and we'll say Arthur Miller lines to each other and then I can work on my operating systems at night."

YAY, NERDS.

But I loved the class so much that my second semester senior year I took another. I started doing stand-up comedy at the U Club. By the time I was sitting where you guys are today, with my CS degree, I had offers from three technology companies to go work for them as a programmer—but I decided instead to move to Chicago, try to get into the improv comedy group Second City, and from there go on to *Saturday Night Live* and ultimate fame and glory.

In the Hollywood version of my story, what would happen is I would move to Chicago for about three minutes, where I would suffer horribly, probably at night or in the rain, and I would come home at night to a dog in a giant loft that I could somehow miraculously afford, and fall asleep. And after those three minutes, I would be discovered by a director who would cast me in a film, and I would walk down the red carpet and my parents would be across the red carpet giving me the thumbs up.

In the real-world story of what happened, when I decided to make a big bet on myself and take this chance because it's what I loved, I was grinding away for a long time, and I had no money, and we would rehearse during the day and perform at night for free. I was taking classes at Second City during the day to try to learn improvisation. Eventually I had to start taking on odd jobs because I had no money, so I put my CS degree from Michigan to use wrapping flatware and selling place settings at Crate and Barrel.

But while I kept on improvising in Chicago for many years, I want to tell you about two lessons I learned there during my first year. The first one was this:

We had this instructor named Don DePaulo. There were four of us up on stage and about ten in the class, and the four on stage were improvising that they were in a Laundromat. The scene ends, and Don asks us, "What do you see up there on that stage right now?" There was nothing up there so we described an empty stage. Don says, "So far today you have improvised that you are in an apartment, an apartment, a Laundromat, and an apartment. What are you guys afraid of?"

We all looked at each other as if to say, "We're not afraid; what do you mean?" He said, "You need to make more courageous choices. The reason the stage is empty and doesn't have a set on it is so you can go out there and be in the Keebler Elf Factory or be on the space shuttle as an astronaut who has never even flown a plane before."

Make courageous choices; take bigger risks.

A couple of months later I was studying with another famous director, named Martin Demont, and Steve Carell was out on stage improvising something. I was backstage and I came up with this amazing line and I thought, "I've gotta get out there and get this line out." So I went out on stage and started trying to move the scene in the direction of what I wanted to say, and Martin stops the scene and says to the whole class (but really he was

talking to me): "You can't plan a script. The beauty of improv is you're experiencing it in the moment. If you try to plan what the next line is going to be, you're just going to be disappointed when the other people don't do or say what you want them to, and you'll stand there frozen." He stopped everyone in the room and said, "Be in this moment."

Now be here in this moment; now be here in this moment.

I stayed in Chicago and improvised for many years, and got auditions for many shows, and got all *none* of them. Fortunately, during this time the Internet happened. That was great because when the Internet happened, I dove in because I saw it as this extensible structure with amazing possibilities. I created a sequence of companies over the course of the next twenty years that led me to Twitter.

If there's ever an example of the importance of making bold bets and focusing on what you love, it's Twitter. When Jack Dorsey talks about the origins of the thinking behind the product, he talks about his fascination with maps, with dispatch systems, and how he took an interest in how they could be made more efficient. When he sent out his first tweet—"just setting up my twttr"— he didn't plan for President Obama to declare victory on that platform in the 2012 election. None of us at Twitter thought that during the earthquake and ensuing tsunami in Fukushima, Japan, that our platform would be a great alternative means of communication if mobile networks were spotty in the aftermath. Certainly none of us even hoped, let alone considered, that our platform would be used to help organize protests across the Middle East and Egypt during the Arab Spring.

Here's the amazing thing about what I've observed from those things. Not only can you not plan the impact you're going to have, you often won't recognize it even while you're having it. A few months after I started at Twitter, Russian President Medvedev was coming to the office. That morning the streets were all completely blocked off and there was U.S. Secret Service and Russian security, so it was a crazy scene. I remember going through the metal detector (that was there just for the day) to get into the office and there were these guys in crazy uniforms and huge dogs—so there was this huge buildup.

President Medvedev came in with his entourage and he was going to send his first tweet from the office, and everyone was waiting for that to happen. As he was taking a tour of the office before sending his first tweet, I get a tap on the shoulder, and this person says to me, "The site is down." Being the thoughtful, charismatic leader that I am I said, ". . . totally down?"

"Totally down."

The next day, you guys and the rest of the world read about President Obama welcoming President Medvedev to Twitter and talking about how perhaps we didn't need the red phone anymore because we could just use Twitter. But for me, that moment was "the site is down." And it's always like that—not the "site is . . ." part. The impact is what others frame for you and the world after it happens. The present is only what you're experiencing and focused on right now.

Every so often my past and present come together. I was invited to a fundraiser at a children's hospital in the Bay Area, and Steve Carell was the guest speaker. So I took a photocopy of the review of the group that Steve and I were in in Chicago over twenty-five years ago to the auction and showed it to him when I got a chance to talk to him. We looked at the review, and talked about the people in the group and where they are now. At the end of that conversation, Steve patted me on the back and said, "I'm really sorry it didn't work out for you."

You cannot draw that path looking forward. You can't draw *any* path looking forward. You have to figure out what you love to do

---

> # The impact is what others frame for you and the world after it happens. The present is only what you're experiencing and focused on right now.

---

and what you have conviction about, and go do that.

Here's the challenge: so far, you guys have gotten where you are by meeting and exceeding expectations. You are awesome; you have excelled. Look at you — you look like an amazing giant choir. But from here on out you have to switch gears. You are no longer meeting and exceeding expectations. There are no expectations; there's no script. When you're doing what you love to do, you become resilient, because you create that habit. You create the habit of taking a gamble on yourself and making courageous choices in service of what you love.

If, on the other hand, you do what you think is expected of

you or what you're supposed to do, and chaos ensues—as it surely will—you will look to external forces for what to do next, because that will be the habit you have created for yourself. You'll be standing there frozen on the stage of your own life. If you're just filling a role, you will be blindsided.

Here's the other problem: I don't feel like I can stand here and tell you to try to have an impact, because the problem seems so massive it seems impossible to have any impact at all, and you end up feeling like you can't do anything. When you think about it, Iran, Syria, North Korea; as you go through that list it makes me want to sweat—and not just because I'm wearing this robe that has no natural fibers in it. (I think it was synthesized from tractor fuel three days ago.)

So instead, what I implore you to do is believe that if you make courageous choices and bet on yourself, and put yourself out there, you will have an impact as a result of those choices, and you don't need to know what that will be or when it will happen because nobody ever does. I like to think of you guys in the metaphor of my early improv days as having been backstage, preparing. And now you are here, and look at everything you've accomplished. You are all so amazing to me and I am so proud of everything you've done. But as you get ready to walk out under the bright lights of the improvisational stage of the rest of your life, I implore you to remember those two lessons I learned years ago.

Be bold; make courageous choices for yourself. Be in the Keebler Elf Factory; what are you afraid of? And secondly, don't always worry about what your next line is supposed to be, or what you're supposed to do next.

There's no script.

Live your life.

Be in this moment; be in this moment; now be in *this* moment.

Twenty years from now, you will be sitting in a different seat in this stadium, and you will be lying in a field looking up at the clouds, and you will be holding a patient's hand walking into surgery, and you will be evaluating a student's essay, and you will be watching your daughter's soccer practice, and you will be standing behind this podium.

Be right there and nowhere else in that moment. Soak it all in, and remember to say "Thank you." Thank you.

⋯ DICK COSTOLO ⋯

is the CEO of Twitter. Before rising to Internet tech stardom, Costolo was a stand-up and improv comedian. He left his comedy career to found several successful tech start-ups, including SpyOnIt and FeedBurner, before taking positions at Google and then Twitter. In 2013, Costolo earned the Crunchies award for "CEO of the Year." He lives in Marin County, California.

Bradley Whitford

UNIVERSITY OF WISCONSIN-MADISON, 2004

A commencement address is what we call in show business a tough gig. You've got a huge room, you've got a big, distracted crowd that thinks they know everything about everything—and probably stayed out a little too late last night celebrating. I heard you at the hotel, by the way. And you've got a bunch of family members of various ages who you have to worry about offending if you happen to get a little too honest.

Somebody once said it's like being the body at a wake. They stick you in the middle of the room, but deep down they really don't want to hear a lot out of you.

The sad truth is, I don't even remember who the speaker was at my graduation. I remember squinting a lot and a vague sense that I would never again be around so many attractive, available young people in my life. It is my solemn duty to inform you that that fear is entirely well-founded. This is coming from a guy who works in Hollywood, by the way.

So I begin this address not only with the full expectation that

I will soon be forgotten, but with the additional humiliation that there will probably be no one there to remind you of who I was.

I just want to take a moment to note that the commencement speaker at Concordia College this year was the president of the United States, George W. Bush. Concordia has about 5,000 students. The University of Wisconsin has about 40,000. Yes, my friends, the question hangs over this beautiful Kohl Center like a foul stench. Why couldn't you get a more significant speaker?

Why would the University of Wisconsin, a school with a reputation and the stature to attract a genuine world leader—at least some uncelebrated public servant . . . the guy who runs the dog pound in Baraboo—somebody, for God's sake! Why would you opt instead for a glorified circus clown from a television show? I can't answer that question, my friends. This is uncomfortable for all of us. I feel your shame.

One thing I can tell you is that Concordia College is getting ripped off. George Bush did not write that speech. No way! A bunch of invisible White House lackeys, otherwise known as speechwriters, wrote it for him. And he just strutted up to the podium, he read it, and then he rode off into the sunset in his little taxpayer-funded 747.

Now, you may think that I am inappropriately taking this opportunity to attack the president on a meaningless issue because of my particular political persuasion—and you would be correct. But I hereby challenge the leader of the free world to swear under oath that he wrote every word of the commencement address that he delivered. It is not gonna happen.

Yes, friends, take solace in the fact that if you had actually paid me anything to come here today, you would be about to get your money's worth. For better or for worse, this horribly disappointing choice of a commencement speaker had to write his own speech.

FALL IN LOVE

with the

PROCESS

and the

RESULTS WILL

FOLLOW.

The first problem I faced when confronted with this grim task was that, as my wife and children will attest, aside from drinking coffee, I have only two areas of expertise—reproduction and acting. Let me begin with the one that I don't mind blabbing about to a room full of strangers—acting.

You know, I get it. I know that it's not the most respectable way to make a living. I am perpetually assaulted by examples of children, quadrupeds, and a wide variety of insufferable idiots who are, on occasion, capable of acting beautifully. This fills my life with bitterness.

The good news is that if you keep at it long enough and you actually get to make a living at this glorified high school extracurricular activity, you not only get a little better at it—given enough chances, even a chimpanzee may type a dictionary—but you begin to see that the process of acting has the potential to show us a little bit about how we might act a little better in our real lives. It comes down to about six basic principles. I call them "Everything I Need to Know in Life I Learned on My Way to a Humiliating Audition," and they go like this:

Number One: Fall in love with the process and the results will follow. You've got to want to act more than you want to be an actor. You've got to want to do whatever you want to do more than you want to be whatever you want to be, want to write more than you want to be a writer, want to heal more than you want to be a doctor, want to teach more than you want to be a teacher, want to serve more than you want to be a politician. Life is too challenging for external rewards to sustain us. The joy is in the journey.

Number Two: Very obvious: do your work. When faced with the terror of an opening night on Broadway, you can either dissolve in a puddle of fear or you can get yourself ready. Drown out your inevitable self-doubt with the work that needs to be done. Find joy in the process of preparation.

Number Three: Once you're prepared, throw your preparation in the trash. The most interesting acting and the most interesting living in this world have the element of surprise and of genuine, honest discovery. Be open to that. You've all spent the majority of your lives in school, where your work is assigned to you and you're supposed to please your teachers.

Once you're prepared, throw your preparation in the trash.

The pressure to get into wonderful institutions like this is threatening to create a generation of what I call hiney-kissing requirement-fulfillers. You are all so much more than that. You've reached the wonderful and terrifying moment where you must be your own guide. Listen to the whispers inside you. We have a lot of problems in this world, and we're going to need you to think outside the box.

Number Four: You are capable of more than you think. If you've ever smashed a mosquito on your arm, there is a murderous Richard III inside you. If you've ever caught your breath at the sight of someone dipping their toes into Lake Mendota in the late afternoon sun over at the Union, you, too, have Romeo's fluttering heart.

Now, I'm not advocating that you all go out and bleach your hair so that you can play the jerk in a really stupid Adam Sandler movie. I don't know what kind of an idiot would think that is a worthwhile way to spend their life. But don't limit yourselves. Take it from the professional extrovert: The most gregarious among us are far more insecure than we would ever admit. We all go through life bristling at our external limitations, but the most difficult chains to break are inside us.

AT THE END OF YOUR DAYS, YOU WILL BE JUDGED BY YOUR GALLOP, NOT BY YOUR STUMBLE.

One of the few graduation speakers who will never be forgotten, Nelson Mandela, put it this way:

"Our worst fear is not that we are inadequate. Our deepest fear is that we are powerful beyond measure. It is our light, not our darkness, that most frightens us. We ask ourselves, 'Who am I to be brilliant, gorgeous, talented, and fabulous?' Actually, who are you not to be? You are a child of God. Your playing small doesn't serve the world."

Let's just take a moment to hope that Nelson Mandela and Adam Sandler never again share a paragraph.[1]

Number Five: Listen. It is the most difficult thing an actor can do, and it is the most riveting. You can't afford to spend your life like a bad actor stumbling through a predetermined performance that is oblivious to the world around you. We can't afford it either. Listening isn't passive. It is an act of liberation that will connect you to the world with compassion and be your best guide as you navigate the choppy waters of love, work, and citizenship.

And finally, Number Six: Take action. Every story you've ever connected with, every leader you've ever admired, every puny little thing that you've ever accomplished is the result of taking action. You have a choice. You can either be a passive victim of circumstance or you can be the active hero of your own life. Action is the antidote to apathy and cynicism and despair. You will inevitably make mistakes. Learn what you can and move on. At the end of your days, you will be judged by your gallop, not by your stumble.

Many of you started here in the fall of 2000. You go out into a world we could not have imagined four years ago. Ominous threats seek to distract us from achieving our spectacular potential as individuals, as a nation, and as a delicate, shrinking planet. We need you.

Come as you are, armed with nothing more than the tools of a mediocre television actor. All we need is for you to find joy in your journey, to find satisfaction in hard work, to be aware of what is happening around you, to free yourself from your imagined limitations, to listen, and finally, to act—not to play make-believe. This isn't a television show. The choices are difficult and the consequences are real.

No matter where you stand politically, we need you to participate in an urgent discussion about the future that we will all share. Some will question your qualifications to participate. We get a lot of that in Hollywood. I like to tell those people that there is nothing less American than telling another American to shut up—so they should shut up.

MAKE YOUR OWN

FUTURE.

MAKE YOUR OWN

HOPE.

MAKE YOUR OWN

LOVE.

This is especially true when the stakes are so high. In the words of the great World War II hero and former U.S. senator George Mc-Govern, "The highest patriotism is not blind allegiance to official policy, but a love of one's country deep enough to hold her to a higher standard."

It has always been up to the people to hold this country up to its spectacular promise. Make no mistake about it—if you choose not to participate at the ballot box or in the urgent discussion about the world that we will one day pass on to the next generation, you no longer live in a democracy. You have sentenced yourself to a civic gulag dictated by the whims of those who choose to participate.

In short, my obnoxiously young friends, you don't just get democracy—you have to make it happen. I urge you to extend that call to action to every aspect of your lives.

Let me be clear—I want you all to stay the hell out of show business. The last thing I need is a bunch of young people invading my job market.

But I do want you to be an actor in your own life. Infuse your life with action. Don't wait for it to happen. Make it happen. Make your own future. Make your own hope. Make your own love. And whatever your beliefs, honor your Creator, not by passively waiting for grace to come down from upon high, but by doing what you can to make grace happen—yourself, right now, right down here on earth.

I will leave you with something I have learned from my only other area of expertise, besides the coffee—being a father. We sit in the shade of trees planted long ago. We have all arrived at this wonderful moment together because of countless gestures of hope made by generations that have preceded us—the baby born, the family begun, the university founded, the care and nurturing of our schools, our communities, a wonderful variety of faiths, and, of course, our families and their families before them.

The line of fire racing across time that we call life is burning brightly in all of you at this moment. We celebrate the joy of your achievement, but we must give thanks for all that brought us here. And we must be keenly aware that our stupendous good fortune carries with it an obligation to keep that flame burning brightly into the future for every living thing that is and is yet to be.

Congratulations, Class of 2004. Go out and plant some trees! Thank you.

1. Since giving this talk, I have discovered that this quote is actually from Marianne Williamson's *A Return to Love* (New York: HarperCollins, 1992) but is often misattributed to Nelson Mandela. Live and learn.

····· BRADLEY WHITFORD ·····

is an American actor with more than eighty acting credits for film and television. He is best known for his role as Deputy Chief of Staff Josh Lyman on *The West Wing*, for which he won the Emmy for Best Supporting Actor in 2001.
He lives in Los Angeles.

Michael Uslan

More than a few years ago, I was sitting right where you are . . . literally in one of those exact same seats out there . . . listening to a graduation speaker proclaim how important it is to succeed in your job. It would have been an inspiring speech except for the fact that neither I nor half my friends had a job lined up by commencement day. Sound familiar to anyone out there?

At my graduation, all I had was a very big dream and a very big question: "Bloomington to Hollywood: How do you get there from here?" I couldn't just declare I wanted to produce the definitive, dark, serious Batman movie and make that leap in a single bound. The problem was: (a) I had no family in the motion picture industry, (b) I had no friends in the motion picture industry, and (c) I didn't come from money, so I couldn't buy my way in.

I had to start on my career path with a series of smaller, achievable goals that could lead me into the world of Batman. I needed something I could do at IU that would get me on the radar in Hollywood and in New York.

Indiana University empowered me to get a job which could eventually lead me to my dream, and it did so by catering to the needs of one individual student. Here's how it happened . . . and believe me, it's hard to believe:

When I was an undergrad, IU had an experimental curriculum department in the College of Arts and Sciences. If you had an idea for a course that was nontraditional and had never been taught before, and if you had the backing of a department, you could appear before a panel of deans and professors to pitch your idea. If they approved it, your course would be accredited and you could teach it on campus.

So, I created a course on comic books, claiming comics to be not only a legitimate American art form as indigenous to this country as jazz, but also as contemporary folklore . . . modern-day mythology. The gods of Egypt, Greece, and Rome still exist, only today they wear capes and spandex.

With the backing of the Folklore Department, I appeared before a panel of professors and deans. I entered a dark, mahogany room with a very long conference table right out of the Justice League's secret sanctum. Now, keep in mind this was the early 1970s. My hair was down to my shoulders, I was wearing a Spider-Man tee shirt, and I think I still had my love beads on.

The professor at the far end of the table looked down at me over those little half-glasses perched on the edge of his nose, and said, "So you're the fellow who wants to teach a course on 'funny books' at my university?" I knew I was in deep . . . trouble.

He let me speak for two minutes and then he cut me off.

I had

TO START ON
MY CAREER PATH
WITH A

SERIES OF
ACHIEVABLE
GOALS.

"Mr. Uslan," he said, "I don't buy your theory. Comic books are cheap entertainment for children. Nothing more. Nothing less. Look, I read them all when I was a kid. I read every issue of *Superman* comics I could get my hands on. But contemporary folklore? Modern-day mythology? I reject your theory."

It was my moment of truth. I inquired if I could ask two questions, and he said I could ask him anything I wanted. So I asked if he was familiar with the story of Moses. He told me he was. I then requested that he very briefly summarize the story of Moses. Eyeing me as if I were insane, he replied that he wasn't sure what game I was playing, but he would play it with me.

The professor said, "The Hebrews were being persecuted; their first-born were being slain. A Hebrew couple placed their infant son in a little wicker basket and sent him down the River Nile, where he was discovered by an Egyptian family who raised him as their own son. When he grew up and learned of his heritage, he became a great hero to his people by . . ." I said, "Thank you. That was great. You mentioned before that you read *Superman* comics as a kid. Do you remember the origin of Superman?" He did. "What's the origin of Superman?" I asked.

The professor said, "The planet Krypton was about to explode. A scientist and his wife placed their infant son in a little rocket ship and sent him to earth. There, he was discovered by the Kents, who raised him as their own son. When he grew up . . ." Suddenly, the professor stopped talking and just stared at me for what seemed like an eternity. He then said, "Your course is accredited."

Oh my God, I would be teaching the world's first accredited comic books course! I'm walking on air back to my apartment when all of a sudden I recall what an IU business prof said to me. He said, "Being creative is not enough. You must market yourself and your ideas if you wish to succeed."

So I picked up a telephone and called United Press International, the huge wire service in Indianapolis. I asked to speak to the reporter who covered education in Indiana. A man got on the phone and I started to scream at him: "What's wrong with you?!? The press is supposed to be the watchdog for the people. I can't believe you're letting them get away with this!"

The reporter pleaded with me to slow down and explain to him what I was talking about. I said, "I hear there's a course on comic books being taught at Indiana University. This is outrageous! Are you telling me as a taxpayer that my money is going to teach our kids 'funny books'?! This must be some Communist plot to infiltrate the youth of America!" And I hung up the phone.

It took this reporter three days to find out if IU really had this course and, if so, who the lunatic was who was teaching it. He came to Bloomington to interview me and then went out with a huge story with photos. It was picked up by almost every newspaper in North America and Europe. From that day on, my phone rang off the hook. Requests for me to appear on radio and TV talk shows. NBC, CBS, and other news crews came to IU and I never once taught a class that wasn't packed with TV cameras and reporters from everything from *Family Weekly* to *Playboy*. I even had my picture appear in *Ripley's Believe It Or Not*. My mother was so proud!

Three weeks later, my phone rings. "Is this Michael Uslan? This is Stan Lee from Marvel Comics in New York." Now for you uninitiated, Stan Lee is the co-creator of Spider-Man, X-Men, Fantastic Four, The Hulk, and the entire pantheon of Marvel superheroes. Hearing Stan's voice over my phone was what I call my very own "Burning Bush" moment. He said, "Mike, everywhere I turn, I see you on TV or in magazines or newspapers. This course you're teaching is great for the entire comic book industry. How can I be helpful?" Not two hours later, the head of DC Comics, publishers of *Superman*, *Batman*, and *Wonder Woman*, calls me. He had special plans to target comic books to college students, and asked if he could fly me to New York to meet.

"Uh . . . okay."

I'm now in New York City at DC Comics, and they offer me a summer job. So, one July day as I'm walking by the office of the editor of a character called The Shadow, I hear him complaining loudly that he has no idea for a *Shadow* script that's due the very next day. Quickly, I poked my head into his office and blurted out, "I have an idea for a story." I didn't. But I realized this was a "moment" . . . a chance to get my foot in the door. Carpe diem. Seize the day. I hemmed and hawed and literally created a story on the spot. The editor told me to have the script on his desk in twenty-four hours and, suddenly, I'm a comic book writer for DC Comics.

Two weeks later, the editor of *Batman* comics passes me by in the hallway. He was very gruff, but once you got to know him, he was a real marshmallow inside. "Hey, kid," he said to me, "I read your *Shadow* script." "You did?" I asked. "Yeah. It didn't stink." "Oh, thank you!" I was beaming. And then he said to me, "How'd you like to take a shot writing *Batman*?"

Since I was eight years old, I dreamed of writing *Batman*. He was my favorite superhero because he had no superpowers. His greatest superpower was his humanity. Plus, he had the best Rogues' Gallery of villains ever! In my heart of hearts, at age eight, I believed that if I studied hard, worked out, and if my dad bought me a cool car, I could be this guy!

Now that my dream of writing *Batman* comics came true, I needed a new dream. While staring out the window of my Bloomington apartment, I decided I wanted to get to Hollywood and produce the dark, serious Batman movie the way he was originally created in 1939—as a creature of the night stalking criminals from the shadows.

The president of DC Comics listened to my goal and tried to give me fatherly advice. "Michael," he said, "since the *Batman* TV show went off the air, no one's been interested in Batman for movies. He's as dead as a dodo. Go get credentials in the film business and then come back and talk to me."

So, every Friday of my senior year, I went to the IU library and read *Variety* magazine; it's the bible of show business. I jotted down the name of every movie and TV executive mentioned in the articles. By the end of the school year, I had the names of 372 people I could send resumes to, instead of having to send out "To Whom It May Concern" letters to personnel departments. And I typed every one of those 372 cover letters with two fingers on a typewriter. Now for those of you who don't know what a typewriter is, visit your local museum. You'll look for it right next to the VCR.

From 372 resumes, I received two job offers: a major New York talent agency invited me to join its agent training program, which would sentence me to two years in their mailroom at $95 per week, and a big-time producer in LA made me an offer to become a production assistant in charge of Xeroxing and going for coffee at a salary of $95 per week. Well, it was time for Plan "B." And if there's no other advice I can give you today, it's always have a Plan "B" . . . and if you can, a Plan "C."

Okay, Plan "B": Unable to get my foot in the door creatively in Hollywood at a pay scale above "starvation," I considered a different route via law school. If I could become an entertainment lawyer as my entrée into the motion picture industry, learn how to finance and produce motion pictures, and meet the power brokers in Hollywood, I could one day sneak in the back door of the creative side.

IU School of Law empowered me by allowing me to take an independent study course because I was the only student in the school interested in entertainment at that time. It was that independent study course that impressed United Artists studio honchos enough to give me, over 200 other applicants, the motion picture production attorney job they had open. Thank you, IU, for yet again accommodating the needs of one individual student.

As part of Plan "B," I stayed at United Artists as if it was graduate school, learning all I could. Then, determined that I would not be trapped into being a lawyer for the rest of my life, I found a partner and mentor in Ben Melniker, the former executive vice president of MGM in its heyday. Together, we raised money, went back to DC with my new credentials, and bought the rights to Batman. Believing I had a 51 percent chance of success with Batman in my pocket, I rolled the dice and quit my job, becoming an independent movie producer by sneaking in the proverbial back door.

I thought everyone in Hollywood would line up to finance my dark, serious vision of Batman. Instead, I was turned down by every single studio in Hollywood. The rejections piled up quickly: "Michael, you're crazy! No one's ever made a movie based on an old TV series. It's never been done!" "Michael, you're insane! Nobody will watch a serious version of Batman. They only remember the pot-bellied funny guy with the Pows! Zaps! And Whams!" "Michael, you're nuts! (Do you see a pattern here by the way?) Your movie, *Batman*, will fail because our movie, *Annie*, didn't do well." I asked this exec if he meant the little red-haired girl who sings, "Tomorrow." He shook his head affirmatively. "But what does she have to do with Batman?" He looked at me and said, "Come on, Michael, they're both out of the 'funny pages.'" That was my rejection. Finally, even good old United Artists turned me down cold when its

DON'T
BELIEVE
THEM

WHEN THEY TELL YOU HOW BAD YOU ARE
AND HOW TERRIBLE YOUR IDEAS ARE.

DOORS WILL SLAM
IN YOUR FACE . . .

GO BACK

AND

KNOCK
AGAIN.

executive said to me, "Michael, you're out of your mind! Batman and Robin will never work as a movie because the movie *Robin and Marian* didn't do well." Now, that film starred Sean Connery and Audrey Hepburn as an aging Robin Hood and Maid Marian. The man apparently turned down *Batman* simply because both movies had the word "Robin" in the title.

From the time we bought the rights to Batman, it took ten years for the film to come out. Ten years! Then it broke one box office record after another, finally prompting my mother to stop asking me, "So when are you going to get a real job?" and it spawned an ongoing worldwide franchise of movies, animation, video games, toys, and best of all, last year's great film made by the genius director Chris Nolan, *Batman Begins*.

There are four simple but critically important lessons I've learned on this journey from Bloomington to Batman, which I'd like to pass along to you at this moment of your graduation:

First, sometimes you have to take calculated risks and roll the dice, or risk growing old and having to say, "I could have been . . ."

Second, you must believe in yourself and in your work. When our first Batman movie broke all those box office records, I received a phone call from that United Artists exec from years before who told me I was out of my mind, that *Robin and Marian* guy. Now he said, "Michael, I'm just calling to congratulate you on *Batman*. I always said you were a visionary." You see the point—don't believe them when they tell you how bad you are and how terrible your ideas are, but also, don't believe them when they start telling you how wonderful you are and how great your ideas are. Just believe in yourself and believe in your work and you'll do just fine. And, don't then forget to market yourself. Use both sides of your brain.

Third, you must have a high threshold for frustration. Take it from the guy who was turned down by every studio in Hollywood. You must knock on doors until your knuckles bleed. Doors will slam in your face; I guarantee it. You must pick yourself up, dust yourself off, and go back and knock again. It's the only way to achieve your goals in life.

Finally, follow whatever your passion is. Do something you love. My dad was a mason, starting at age sixteen, when he dropped out of school to help his family survive the Depression. Until he was eighty he worked six days a week no matter how hot or how cold out it was outside. He was an Old World artist . . . a real craftsman who created magnificent fireplaces and homes out of bricks and stones. Every morning of my childhood, I saw my dad jump out of bed before dawn, eager to get to work, a smile on his face. He was doing what he loved, and I knew that was what I wanted out of life . . . to be able to wake up on a rainy Monday morning and be able to say, "Boy, I can't wait to get to work!" But I had to find my own bricks and stones. Today, I challenge you to find yours.

If there's one quotation that sums up my journey through life and the choices I've made, it's the closing lines of a poem by Robert Frost, which I now pass along to you:

"I shall be telling this with a sigh / Somewhere ages and ages hence: / Two roads diverged in a wood, and I— / I took the one less traveled by, / And that has made all the difference."

Bats of luck, every one of you, and congratulations!

····· **MICHAEL USLAN** ·····

is the originator and executive producer of the
Batman/Dark Knight movie franchise and, most
recently, executive producer of *The Lego Movie*.
His memoir, *The Boy Who Loved Batman*,
is published by Chronicle Books.

Tom Wolfe

BOSTON UNIVERSITY, 2000

Note: When Boston University presented Tom Wolfe with an honorary Doctor of Humane Letters degree, Chancellor John Silber and President Jon Westling also presented him with a red-trimmed white academic gown, to go along with his customary white suit. Mr. Wolfe was suitably surprised.

'm telling you [looking down at the white gown that now surmounts his white silk suit] this is a total surprise. I knew something had irresistibly drawn me to this moment—and there you have it! This is absolutely . . . well . . . there is no university to which I would rather have been invited on this day in this May, whose hood I would rather wear and, as it now turns out, whose raiment I would rather wear, than Boston University. Thanks to a couple of Johns, John Silber and Jon Westling, and to a brilliant faculty, some of whom we've met at this podium this morning, this university has been a shining lighthouse of independent thought and of liberal democracy in the classical meaning of "liberal" as John Silber has so wonderfully defined it over the years. I choose the image of a lighthouse very carefully, John and Jon, because

LIGHTHOUSES

are

BUILT TO
STAND ALONE

and to

BEAR THE BRUNT
OF THE STORM

NO MATTER WHAT THAT
STORM MAY BE.

lighthouses are built to stand alone and to bear the brunt of the storm, no matter what that storm may be.

Having said that, I want to offer my congratulations to the class of 2000 and to their families. As someone who grew up in the Great Depression of the 1930s, I know that a commencement is a family triumph. Forget money. Aside from love, the cardinal virtues, and time, there is no greater gift parents can give a child than an education at a place like Boston University.

I feel a little bit like Sigourney Weaver, who gave the commencement address at my daughter's high school a couple of years ago. It's an all-girl school, and Sigourney Weaver said, "My intention this morning was to talk to you girls about boys. But the headmistress informs me I only have fifteen minutes. So instead I'm going to tell you the meaning of life."

Unfortunately I don't remember what the meaning was, because she kept me in stitches for fifteen minutes, and I forgot. So in the few minutes I have with you, I'm just going to tell you one thing that I wish that somebody had told me when I was in your shoes forty-nine years ago, graduating from college. (Actually, to be a graduate of the year 2000 has a much better ring to it than to be a graduate from the class of 1951. We did the best we could, but, what can you do with "1951"?) And this one thing is even more virulent today than it was half a century ago: it's the fact that we live in an age in which ideas, important ideas, are worn like articles of fashion—and for precisely the same reason articles of fashion are worn, which is to make the wearer look better and to feel à la mode.

Let me give you an example: There's a very fashionable idea right now that each people, each culture, has its own integrity, has its own validity, which must be respected and must have its day in the sun. I don't think anybody will bother to argue with that. But what I think you're going to find fairly soon, as you head out into the world, are two things: first, that it's irrelevant, and second, that it leads to what I think of as "pernicious enlightenment."

Consider this specific case, which is reasonably local: Seven years ago the mayor of New York City came to Boston. He hired away your police commissioner, William Bratton, and brought him to New York to see if he couldn't do something about crime in New York, which had reached horrendous proportions. William Bratton did a very daring thing. He reversed the usual procedure. He said, "We will reduce the incidence of major crimes by going after the so-called 'quality of life' crimes, misdemeanors that have been considered so minor in the face of shootings, muggings, beatings, stabbings, that police departments are barely paying attention to them anymore. We are going to create and establish a sense of order in New York City. We are going to take back the streets. And that's going to have consequences you can't even imagine." And that was what happened. Overnight, William Bratton engineered the most dramatic reduction in crime in any large city in the history of the United States.

How? For one thing, he started enforcing laws against truancy that hadn't been enforced for seventy-five years. Police started picking up thirteen-, fourteen-, fifteen-year-old children who were out on the streets in the middle of the day, and they told them, "You're supposed to be in school." In two months the rate of juvenile delinquency in New York City dropped 75 percent. Because what do you do if you are thirteen, fourteen, fifteen, you're not in school, you're out all day? You dream up mischief and get into trouble, that's what you do. Bratton decided to enforce the law against riding the subways for free by jumping the turnstiles. If you've ever been on a

New York City subway, you know the turnstiles are about the same height as one of those leather horses you use in gymnastics. By 1993 a whole generation of young people in New York was vaulting turnstiles. They had become absolutely Olympic about it. I mean, many, many would vault and do a flip in the air. That was cool. I saw a kid one day do a one-and-a-half gainer. I am not exaggerating! A one-and-a-half gainer! That's fun and games, but what is the impression this makes on everybody else? "I'm an idiot. I obeyed the law. I'm an idiot. The subways belong to the lawless. The city is unraveling." The police began arresting them—and this had an unanticipated dividend: 30 percent of the jumpers had outstanding warrants for more serious crimes.

Well, now we get to the boom boxes. Under William Bratton, the New York City Police Department identified 227 boom-box hot spots. Now, when I talk about boom boxes, I'm not talking about these radio and CD players that you see boys carrying on their shoulders—nothing that simple. These hot spots had to do with cars. Boys would take the back seat out of their cars, put in a piece of plywood from the base of the front seat right up to the rear window, and put in two twenty-inch speakers. Twenty-inch speakers create so much heat they would have to take everything out of the trunk and put in fans to cool off the equipment. I got curious and I went out, and I've been in these cars when they are going full blast. The tympanum will make your ears flap! I'm not kidding you.

All right, so here you've got the set-up. Now, here's the kind of song that would come booming out at midnight in 227 residential neighborhoods in New York. The words are a bit crude about the edges, but to give you the flavor I have to use them. This is a song called "Death on the Installment Plan" by a group called the Child Abusers:

\

Nine to five you park yo' butt
Beneath the bitch box
    on the wall
And lap up all that crap inside
The rut they make you crawl.
So yo', go buy yo' own death, bro,
And die on the
      installment plan,
'Fo they cut yo' nuts and hang you
From the necktie on
    the bald man.

Now, you have to imagine that being sung not by me but by four bawling twenty-year-olds with electric guitars, electric bass, and reverbo-amped drums over twenty-inch speakers in somebody's neighborhood at midnight, one, two, or three in the morning. So the police started cracking down on that, and one young man fought the case in court and lost. He then appealed, and the appeals court reversed the decision with the following logic: "What is too loud in one culture is not too loud in another." Now, think what that means. I do not know that boy's background, but all I can say is, how condescending can you get? What sort of pernicious enlightenment leads a panel of judges to assume that somebody's culture finds it acceptable to listen to the Child Abusers singing "Death on the Installment Plan" at 180 decibels in their neighborhoods in the middle of the night?

The truth is that there is a common bond among all cultures, among all peoples in this world . . . at least among those who have reached the level of the wheel, the shoe, and the toothbrush.

And that common bond is that much-maligned class known as the bourgeoisie—the middle class. These people are to be found not only in Boston, they are to be found in Bombay; in Benin City in Benin, West Africa; in Bonn in what used to be called West Germany; in Beirut; in Bermuda; in Barcelona. They are all over the world, in every continent, every nation, every society, every culture, everywhere you find the wheel, the shoe, and the toothbrush, and wherever they are, all of them believe in the same things. And what are those things? Peace, order, education, hard work, initiative, enterprise, creativity, cooperation, looking out for one another, looking out for the future of children, patriotism, fair play, and honesty. How much more do you want from the human beast? How much more can you possibly expect?

HOW MUCH MORE DO YOU WANT FROM THE HUMAN BEAST? HOW MUCH MORE CAN YOU POSSIBLY EXPECT?

I say that the middle class around the world—and it certainly flowers in this country—is the highest form of evolution. The bourgeoisie!—the human beast doesn't get any better! The worldwide bourgeoisie makes what passes today for aristocrats—people consumed by juvenility who hang loose upon society—look like shiftless children.

And we writers spent the entire twentieth century tearing down the bourgeoisie! The great H. L. Mencken, probably the most brilliant American essayist of the twentieth century, started it with his term "the booboisie." Then Sherwood Anderson in *Winesburg, Ohio* presented us with the oh-so proper, oh-so twisted Midwestern preacher who in fact is a Peeping Tom. That formula has now been ground out and ground out and ground out until it takes the form of movies like *American Beauty*. We in the arts have been complicit in the denigration of the best people on earth. Why? Because so many of the most influential ideas of our time are the product of a new creature of the twentieth century, a creature that did not exist until 1898—and that creature is known as "the intellectual."

Now, we must be careful to make a distinction between the intellectual and the person of intellectual achievement. The two are very, very different animals. There are people of intellectual achievement who increase the sum of human knowledge, the powers of human insight, and analysis. And then there are the intellectuals. An intellectual is a person knowledgeable in one field who speaks out only in others. Starting in the early twentieth century, for the first time an ordinary storyteller, a novelist, a short story writer, a poet, a playwright, in certain cases a composer, an artist, or even an opera singer could achieve a tremendous eminence by becoming morally indignant about some public issue. It required no intellectual effort whatsoever. Suddenly he was elevated to a plane from which he could look down upon ordinary people. Conversely—this fascinates me—conversely, if you are merely a brilliant scholar, merely someone who has added immeasurably to the sum of human knowledge and the powers of human insight, that does not qualify you for the eminence of being an intellectual.

I'll give you an example right across the river (I think I'm pointing in the right direction) [points over shoulder to the northeast]. I'm standing right near where Pete Suder used to play second base for the Boston Braves. Anyway, right across the river there is the amazing figure of Noam Chomsky. Noam Chomsky on his own did an extremely brilliant thing. He's a linguist; he's a scientist and a scholar. He figured out on his own that speech, grammar, and the human capacity to record in memory are literally, physically, built into the human nervous system. It is not something learned; it is built in. That is why a child can take a new word like "chair" and immediately drop it into a sentence at the age of two and say, "My doll fell off the chair," a whole sentence with a subject, a predicate, an object. It's only in our time, the end of the twentieth century, the beginning of the twenty-first, that neuroscientists have the instruments by which they are beginning to prove that Noam Chomsky was right. A brilliant, brilliant human being. Did anyone call him an intellectual merely because he was one of the most brilliant people in the United States? No. When did he become an intellectual? When he finally spoke out concerning something he knew absolutely nothing about: the war in Vietnam. When he denounced the war in Vietnam, Chomsky put on the requisite display of utter ignorance—and thereby became a leading American intellectual.

One of the things that I find really makes it worth watching all the Academy Awards, all the Emmys, all those awards ceremonies, is to see how today's actors and television performers have discovered the formula. If you become indignant, this elevates you to the plane of "intellectual." No mental activity is required. It is a rule, to which there has never been an exception, that when an actor or a television performer rises up to the microphone at one of these awards ceremonies and expresses moral indignation over something, he illustrates Marshall McLuhan's dictum that "moral indignation is a standard strategy for endowing the idiot with dignity."

Another rule without a single exception is that the intellectual always averts his eyes from the obvious when the subject is the United States. This country, in our time, has fulfilled the dream of the utopian socialists of the nineteenth century, the Saint-Simons, the Fouriers. This is the first country on earth in which the ordinary working man has the political freedom, the personal freedom, the free time, the money, the wherewithal to express himself in any way that he may want, so that you may be sure that today, as we convene here in the former Braves Field—Pete Suder Land—now Nickerson Field at Boston University—you may be sure that your Cablevision lineman or your air conditioning mechanic or your burglar alarm repairman is right now in Puerto Vallarta or Barbados or Saint Kitts, and he's there with his third wife (they're expensive, divorces are), and right now the two of them are out on the terrace of some resort hotel. He's wearing his Ricky Martin cane-cutter shirt, open down to the sternum, the better to allow the gold chains to twinkle in his chest hairs, and he and his wife have just ordered a little round of Quibell sparkling water . . . because Perrier and San Pelegrino are so tacky by now, you know. . . . One can't even use the old term "working class" anymore, much less "proletariat." Your plumber, your electrician, is now part of the highest form of the evolution of the species, the bourgeoisie American-style.

Here we are on the verge of a second American Century. We've just completed the first American Century, in which we achieved a power that would have made Julius Caesar twitch with envy.

YOU'RE GOING TO
HAVE TO

MAKE

THE

CRUCIAL

JUDGMENTS

YOURSELVES.

And ours has been a largely benign power. We saved the world from two bands of slave-hunting predators, the German Nazis and the Russian Communists, two barbaric hordes who made the Huns and Magyars of yore seem whimsical by comparison. At the same time we opened our arms to people from all over the earth, from every country, every culture, every religion, every conceivable background. Why don't we build a second Statue of Liberty? What we did in the twentieth century was fantastic. People from Eritrea, from Ethiopia, from Guyana, from Cambodia, from Vietnam, refugees from all over the world—we welcomed them! This is the only country in the world where such a triumph of first-generation immigrants could take place, and God bless us for the fact that we are this open to the people of the entire world.

We are in the beginning of what may be a Pax Americana, the equivalent of the Pax Romana that began two millennia ago. This may be the second century of a thousand years of rule in the world by a benign liberal democracy. I think we should rejoice in this. And I feel so much better knowing that there are people like yourselves, members of the class of 2000 at Boston University, who have developed the independence of thought to judge the world strictly by the evidence of your own eyes. You're not going to find many traditional judges who can lead you any longer, since they now wander helplessly, bemused by the willful ignorance of that bizarre twentieth-century organism, the intellectual. You're going to have to make the crucial judgments yourselves. But you are among the very handful of those who can do it. You are graduates of one of the two or three greatest universities in America. You have been raised in, you have been developed in, a tradition of straight thinking and straight talking. You have been taught to lead your lives in the tradition of those who, in the great phrase of a great writer and a great leader, John Silber, are straight shooters.

God bless you all, and best of luck, and thank you so much for letting me be a part of the commencement of Boston University's Class of 2000.

⸱⸱⸱⸱⸱ TOM WOLFE ⸱⸱⸱⸱⸱

is the acclaimed author of many books, including *The Kandy-Kolored Tangerine-Flake Streamline Baby*, *The Electric Kool-Aid Acid Test*, *The Pump House Gang*, *The Right Stuff*, *A Man in Full*, and *The Bonfire of the Vanities*. He has reported for the *Washington Post*, the *New York Herald Tribune*, and *New York* magazine and is considered one of the founders of New Journalism. Among his many accolades are a National Book Award and the 2010 National Book Foundation Medal for Distinguished Contribution to American Letters. He lives in New York City.

Madeleine L'Engle
WELLESLEY COLLEGE, 1991

I t is a very special pleasure for me to be here at Wellesley College today, a pleasure that goes back to my childhood.

I was born on the island of Manhattan and grew up in New York, a solitary, only child, with parents almost old enough to be my grandparents, with full lives of their own, so when I wasn't in school I had a lot of time to myself. When I was in fourth grade I was put into a school which is still in existence, so it will be nameless, which was supposed to be one of the best schools in the city. In that school it was very important that one be good at sports. One of my legs was longer than the other—still is—so I was clumsy and not a good runner. Any team which had the misfortune to have me on its side automatically lost. The kids would choose sides, and the unlucky team to get me would let out anguished groans, and I can't blame them. I was hardly an asset to team sports. However, for some reason which is still not clear to me, my homeroom teacher decided that since I couldn't run relay races, I wasn't very bright. She simply accepted the other students' assessment of me, and I couldn't do anything right. I quickly learned that there was no point in doing homework for her, because she was going to hold it up in ridicule to the class, or put it down. So I would go home and dump down my school books and not look at them again, say wryly to myself that I was the dumb one, the unpopular one, and then I would move into the real world, where I read stories, wrote stories, and tried in my own way to find out what human relationships were all about.

NO MATTER WHAT IT COST I WAS GOING TO STAY ON THE SIDE OF TRUTH.

It was also in fourth grade that I learned about the perfidy of the adult world, and the earlier this is learned the better; it can come as a terrible shock if it doesn't hit you til later. I learned it in French class, which was being taught by a very large Frenchwoman. I needed to be excused, and I raised my hand, and my French teacher wouldn't let me leave the room. Three times I raised my hand, each time a little more desperately than the time before, and three times she refused to let me go. When the bell rang I ran, and I didn't make it. Now, to wet your pants in fourth grade is really pretty horrendous. My mother came for me, and here was this little wet mess. I told her what had happened, and she went to the principal. The principal called in the French teacher, and the French teacher said, "Well, Madeleine never asked to be excused. Of course if she'd raised her hand I'd have let her go. She's just ashamed of wetting her pants, a big girl like that. Tell her not to lie about it next time." So there was a grown-up lying, and being believed, and I, only a child, was not. And that made me determined never to be like that French teacher. No matter what it cost I was going to stay on the side of truth.

The next year there was a poetry contest which was open to the entire school, and judged by the head of the English department. The entries weren't screened, or I'd never have got one in. My poem won the contest, and my homeroom teacher predictably said, "Madeleine couldn't possibly have written that poem. She's not very bright, you know. She must have copied it from someplace."

So my mother went up to school, bearing the large body of work I had produced when I should have been doing homework, and it had to be conceded that Madeleine could have written that poem after all.

I was taken out of that school and sent to another, where I had a homeroom teacher on her very first teaching job. She was the first person to see any potential in this shy, awkward child. She affirmed me, gave me extra work to do. I remember she had me write a sequel to the *Odyssey*, with Telemachus as the hero. Her honoring of me helped the other students to see me as something more than the girl who was bad at relay races. I didn't have instant popularity, but I began to make friends. I did my homework with enthusiasm, because my teacher challenged me.

Her name was Margaret Clapp, and she was to become the eighth president of Wellesley. So I had the benefit of being taught by a woman who was not only a great educator, but a great person, and perhaps it is only a great educator who understands that part of education is affirming each person she encounters as being intrinsically valuable. My previous teachers had estimated me as

I LEARNED TO BE

WILLING
TO BE WHO
I WAS, NOT

THE PLASTIC MODEL OF

WHO I HAD
THOUGHT

I WANTED TO BE.

worthless; Miss Clapp gave me a sense of value, that it was all right to be me, that my lack of athletic skills was more than compensated for by other skills, that imagination was important.

Miss Clapp also helped me into a creative realism. I gave up some impossible dreams of making the longest or the highest jumps in gym; I accepted that I had a bad knee and that this would prevent me from being a great athlete, but I also accepted that not everybody has to be a great athlete. I learned to be willing to be who I was, not the plastic model of who I had thought I wanted to be. It was not that I didn't attempt the impossible. I did. But it was the impossible in areas where I already showed promise. My sequel to the *Odyssey* was probably pretty terrible, but it was a good example of the right kind of impossible, the impossible that called into play the gifts I already had, the gift of gab, the gift of putting words together articulately, the gift of imagination.

I hope that you have encountered teachers who understand the importance of imagination, that part of the brain which goes beyond cognition to intuition. An article in the *New York Times* dealt with the discovery that there is far more to the brain than the conscious part which is concerned with facts and proof, and that many, if not most, major discoveries have been made with the intuitive part of the brain when the scientist is thinking but has relaxed, so that the whole brain can work and not just the conscious, controllable area.

Of course this is a masculine discovery, new to the male of the species but not to the female. Women have been allowed by society to be far more whole than men; we have not been forced to repress our inner selves, our intuitive, imaginative, numinous side. We have been allowed to go down into the darkness of unexpectedness, whereas men have been forced by society to limit themselves to the reasonable, the rational, the provable.

I, too, went to a women's college, Smith College. One great advantage of a women's college is that whatever there is to be done, we women do. If there is a magazine to be started, we start it. If there is an officer to be elected, one of us will be elected. I left college and went to New York to earn my living with the assurance that all doors were of course open to me, and that's a good attitude to have. If you expect doors to be open, they're likely to be open. If you expect them to be closed, they're likely to slam in your face. And I left college having majored in English literature, having spent four years with great writers, with an understanding that intellect and intuition were equally important.

In Greek mythology the intellect is masculine, Apollo driving the chariot of the sun across the sky, whereas wisdom is feminine, Sophia, or better, Hagia Sophia, holy wisdom. It is quite possible to be intellectual without any wisdom whatsoever, and this is always disastrous. And wisdom without intellect can be too otherworldly to be effective. It is when the two work together that true maturity can be realized. It is when the two work together that our wonderful minds can turn us towards truth. Intellect alone wants facts, provable facts; intellect working with wisdom can understand that truth goes far beyond and transcends facts. One of my early home-room teachers accused me of "telling a story." She was not complimenting me on my fertile imagination; she was making the deadly accusation that I was telling a lie. It is only when the brain is limited to the cognitive alone that story can be confused with untruth, whereas story is one of the most potent vehicles of truth available to the human being.

Now, when I am talking about male and female I am not talking about men versus women, because we all have a marvelous combination of male and female within us, and part of maturing is learning to balance these two components so that they are the most fertile. It is only then that we are able to make creative choices and to understand that we do indeed have choices.

I have had the pleasure of living with my two granddaughters during their college years, and not long ago we were having dinner with several of their classmates, and one young woman said that their women's studies professor had told them that any woman who married and had children and who wrote was a martyr. My granddaughter, Charlotte, looked at me, asking, "Gran, were you a martyr?" I replied, "No, Charlotte, I was not a martyr. I chose my own conflicts. They were indeed conflicts, but I chose them. No one forced me to marry, to have children, to continue to go on writing. It was my free choice. So there's no way I could be a martyr."

Don't fall into martyrdom! That's a choice too. So is being a victim. I don't like that word. When bad things happen it is up to me to choose to be a victim or to get on with it. Terrible things can happen to us: rape, accident, bereavement; life is precarious and full of the unexpected, but we do not have to become victims, no matter what happens. That is a choice, and one we do not have to make. If we chose to remain ourselves, full of potential, then we can take whatever happens and redeem it by openness, courage, and willingness to move on. As women it is our responsibility to use all parts of ourselves, male and female, intellect and intuition, conscious and subconscious minds.

From my college reading of Aristotle's *Poetics* I remember particularly this phrase—"That which is plausible and impossible is better than that which is possible and implausible"—and that has had a profound effect on my adult life. When we believe in the impossible, it becomes possible, and we can do all kinds of extraordinary things. We can balance the male and female within us like

NOTHING THAT'S EASY IS REALLY WORTH VERY MUCH

an acrobat in the circus, and that balancing act is one of the most important choices open to us. We can dare to enter the vulnerable intimacy of friendship and love. Some of you will choose the underrated job of homemaker, of wife and mother. Some of you will go single-mindedly after a career. Some of you, like me, will make the difficult choice of choosing both but then, as I used to tell my children, nothing that's easy is really worth very much, and just because it's difficult is no reason not to try.

Remember that one of the glories of being human is that we are fallible. We are the creatures who learn by making mistakes. I don't know about you, but I learn by what I do wrong, not by what I do right. An ant does not have this privilege. In ant societies if an ant deviates from the pattern that ant is a goner. Ants do not have the freedom of choice that we have.

So my hope for all of you is that you have been affirmed as valuable during these college years, and that you leave here knowing who you are, what your strengths are, and what your weaknesses are, and that the greatest human beings are a marvelous mixture of both. I hope that you know that you have choices, and that you have the freedom to discover what is true for you, and to follow that choice. Miss Clapp gave me the gift of being willing to know myself, with realism and with hope. She was the first person to help me to know where and how I could break through the possible to the impossible, and to understand that it is when we plunge into something difficult that we are given whatever tools we need. She helped to start me on what has been and is still a fascinating journey, full of unexpected joys and sorrows and challenges. So I hope the same for you, that you will use fully the Apollo, the intellect, which is a great glory, and rejoice equally in Sophia, the wisdom which makes the intellect creative instead of destructive. Women are needed in a world which is hung up on the literal, the provable. So go out there with courage and imagination and be fully whoever you are, because that is who you are meant to be. Then the impossible becomes possible, and you will give hope wherever you are.

Go, and God bless you.

······ MADELEINE L'ENGLE ······

(1918–2007) wrote the Newbery Medal–winning novel *A Wrinkle in Time* and its sequels, the Time series, which include National Book Award winner *A Swiftly Tilting Planet*. She received the Margaret Edwards Award for lifetime achievement from the American Library Association.

Michael Lewis

PRINCETON UNIVERSITY, 2012

Thirty years ago I sat where you sat. I must have listened to some older person share his life experience. But I don't remember a word of it. I can't even tell you who spoke. What I do remember, vividly, is graduation. I'm told you're meant to be excited, perhaps even relieved, and maybe all of you are. I wasn't. I was totally outraged. Here I'd gone and given them four of the best years of my life and this is how they thanked me for it. By kicking me out.

At that moment I was sure of only one thing: I was of no possible economic value to the outside world. I'd majored in art history, for a start. Even then this was regarded as an act of insanity. I was almost certainly less prepared for the marketplace than most of you. Yet somehow I have wound up rich and famous. Well, sort of. I'm going to explain, briefly, how that happened. I want you to understand just how mysterious careers can be, before you go out and have one yourself.

I graduated from Princeton without ever having published a word of anything, anywhere. I didn't write for the *Prince*, or for anyone else. But at Princeton, studying art history, I felt the first twinge of literary ambition. It happened while working on my senior thesis. My adviser was a truly gifted professor, an archaeologist named William Childs. The thesis tried to explain how the Italian sculptor Donatello used Greek and Roman sculpture—which is actually totally beside the point, but I've always wanted to tell someone. God knows what Professor Childs actually thought of it, but he helped me to become engrossed. More than engrossed: obsessed. When I handed it in I knew what I wanted to do for the rest of my life: to write senior theses. Or, to put it differently: to write books.

I did what everyone does who has no idea what to do with themselves: I went to graduate school. I wrote at night, without much effect, mainly because I hadn't the first clue what I should write about.

Then I went to my thesis defense. I listened and waited for Professor Childs to say how well written my thesis was. He didn't. And so after about forty-five minutes I finally said, "So. What did you think of the writing?"

"Put it this way," he said. "Never try to make a living at it."

And I didn't—not really. I did what everyone does who has no idea what to do with themselves: I went to graduate school. I wrote at night, without much effect, mainly because I hadn't the first clue what I should write about. One night I was invited to a dinner, where I sat next to the wife of a big shot at a giant Wall Street investment bank called Salomon Brothers. She more or less forced her husband to give me a job. I knew next to nothing about Salomon Brothers. But Salomon Brothers happened to be where Wall Street was being reinvented—into the place we have all come to know and love. When I got there I was assigned, almost arbitrarily, to the very best job in which to observe the growing madness: They turned me into the house expert on derivatives. A year and a half later Salomon Brothers was handing me a check for hundreds of thousands of dollars to give advice about derivatives to professional investors.

Now I had something to write about: Salomon Brothers. Wall Street had become so unhinged that it was paying recent Princeton graduates who knew nothing about money small fortunes to pretend to be experts about money. I'd stumbled into my next senior thesis.

I called up my father. I told him I was going to quit this job that now promised me millions of dollars to write a book for an advance of forty grand. There was a long pause on the other end of the line. "You might just want to think about that," he said.

"Why?"

"Stay at Salomon Brothers ten years, make your fortune, and then write your books," he said.

I didn't need to think about it. I knew what intellectual passion felt like—because I'd felt it here, at Princeton—and I wanted to feel it again. I was twenty-six years old. Had I waited until I was thirty-six, I would never have done it. I would have forgotten the feeling.

SUCCESS

IS

always

RATIONALIZED.

The book I wrote was called *Liar's Poker*. It sold a million copies. I was twenty-eight years old. I had a career, a little fame, a small fortune, and a new life narrative. All of a sudden people were telling me I was born to be a writer. This was absurd. Even I could see there was another, truer narrative, with luck as its theme. What were the odds of being seated at that dinner next to that Salomon Brothers lady? Of landing inside the best Wall Street firm from which to write the story of an age? Of landing in the seat with the best view of the business? Of having parents who didn't disinherit me but instead sighed and said, "Do it if you must?" Of having had that sense of must kindled inside me by a professor of art history at Princeton? Of having been let into Princeton in the first place?

This isn't just false humility. It's false humility with a point. My case illustrates how success is always rationalized. People really don't like to hear success explained away as luck—especially successful people. As they age, and succeed, people feel their success was somehow inevitable. They don't want to acknowledge the role played by accident in their lives. There is a reason for this: The world does not want to acknowledge it either.

I wrote a book about this, called *Moneyball*. It was ostensibly about baseball, but was in fact about something else. There are poor teams and rich teams in professional baseball, and they spend radically different sums of money on their players. When I wrote my book the richest team in professional baseball, the New York Yankees, was then spending about $120 million on its twenty-five players. The poorest team, the Oakland A's, was spending about $30 million. And yet the Oakland team was winning as many games as the Yankees—and more than all the other, richer teams.

This isn't supposed to happen. In theory, the rich teams should buy the best players and win all the time. But the Oakland team had figured something out: The rich teams didn't really understand who the best baseball players were. The players were misvalued. And the biggest single reason they were misvalued was that the experts did not pay sufficient attention to the role of luck in baseball success. Players got given credit for things they did that depended on the performance of others: Pitchers got paid for winning games, hitters got paid for knocking in runners on base. Players got blamed and credited for events beyond their control. Where balls that got hit happened to land on the field, for example.

Forget baseball, forget sports. Here you had these corporate employees, paid millions of dollars a year. They were doing exactly the same job that people in their business had been doing forever. In front of millions of people who evaluate their every move. They had statistics attached to everything they did. And yet they were misvalued—because the wider world was blind to their luck.

This had been going on for a century. Right under all of our noses. And no one noticed—until it paid a poor team so well to notice that they could not afford not to notice. And you have to ask: If a professional athlete paid millions of dollars can be misvalued, who can't be? If the supposedly pure meritocracy of professional sports can't distinguish between lucky and good, who can?

The *Moneyball* story has practical implications. If you use better data, you can find better values; there are always market inefficiencies to exploit, and so on. But it has a broader and less practical message: Don't be deceived by life's outcomes. Life's outcomes, while not entirely random, have a huge amount of luck baked into them. Above all, recognize that if you have had success, you have also had luck—and with luck comes obligation. You owe a debt, and not just to your gods. You owe a debt to the unlucky.

YOU
OWE
A
DEBT
TO THE
UNLUCKY.

Life's outcomes,

WHILE NOT ENTIRELY RANDOM,

have a huge amount of

LUCK

BAKED INTO THEM.

I make this point because—along with this speech—it is something that will be easy for you to forget.

I now live in Berkeley, California. A few years ago, just a few blocks from my home, a pair of researchers in the Cal psychology department staged an experiment. They began by grabbing students, as lab rats. Then they broke the students into teams, segregated by sex. Three men, or three women, per team. Then they put these teams of three into a room, and arbitrarily assigned one of the three to act as leader. Then they gave them some complicated moral problem to solve: say, what should be done about academic cheating, or how to regulate drinking on campus.

Exactly thirty minutes into the problem solving, the researchers interrupted each group. They entered the room bearing a plate of cookies. Four cookies. The team consisted of three people, but there were these four cookies. Every team member obviously got one cookie, but that left a fourth cookie, just sitting there. It should have been awkward. But it wasn't. With incredible consistency the person arbitrarily appointed leader of the group grabbed the fourth cookie and ate it. Not only ate it, but ate it with gusto: lips smacking, mouth open, drool at the corners of their mouths. In the end all that was left of the extra cookie were crumbs on the leader's shirt.

This leader had performed no special task. He had no special virtue. He'd been chosen at random, thirty minutes earlier. His status was nothing but luck. But it still left him with the sense that the cookie should be his.

This experiment helps to explain Wall Street bonuses and CEO pay, and I'm sure lots of other human behavior. But it also is relevant to new graduates of Princeton University. In a general sort of way you have been appointed the leader of the group. Your appointment may not be entirely arbitrary. But you must sense its arbitrary aspect: You are the lucky few. Lucky in your parents, lucky in your country, lucky that a place like Princeton exists that can take in lucky people, introduce them to other lucky people, and increase their chances of becoming even luckier. Lucky that you live in the richest society the world has ever seen, in a time when no one actually expects you to sacrifice your interests to anything.

All of you have been faced with the extra cookie. All of you will be faced with many more of them. In time you will find it easy to assume that you deserve the extra cookie. For all I know, you may. But you'll be happier, and the world will be better off, if you at least pretend that you don't.

Never forget: in the nation's service. In the service of all nations.

Thank you.

And good luck.

····· **MICHAEL LEWIS** ·····

is the bestselling author of *The Blind Side*,
Flash Boys, *The Big Short*, *Boomerang*, *Moneyball*,
The New New Thing, *Coach*, *Losers*, and *Liar's Poker*,
among others. *The Blind Side* and *Moneyball* were
both adapted into Academy Award–nominated films.
Lewis is a columnist for *Bloomberg News*, and
he has contributed to *Vanity Fair*, the *New York
Times Magazine*, *Slate*, *Sports Illustrated*, and
The Spectator. He lives in Berkeley, California.

Nora Ephron
WELLESLEY COLLEGE, 1996

President Walsh, trustees, faculty, friends, noble parents . . . and dear class of 1996, I am so proud of you. Thank you for asking me to speak to you today. I had a wonderful time trying to imagine who had been ahead of me on the list and had said no; I was positive you'd have to have gone to Martha Stewart first. And I meant to call her to see what she would have said, but I forgot. She would probably be up here telling you how to turn your lovely black robes into tents. I will try to be at least as helpful, if not quite as specific as that.

I'm very conscious of how easy it is to let people down on a day like this, because I remember my own graduation from Wellesley very, very well, I am sorry to say. The speaker was Santha Rama Rau, who was a woman writer, and I was going to be a woman writer. And in fact, I had spent four years at Wellesley going to lectures by women writers hoping that I would be the beneficiary of some terrific secret—which I never was. And now here I was at graduation, under these very trees, absolutely terrified. Something was over. Something safe and protected. And something else was about to begin. I was heading off to New York, and I was sure that I would live there forever and never meet anyone and end up dying one of those New York deaths where no one even notices you're missing until the smell drifts into the hallway weeks later. And I sat here thinking, "OK, Santha, this is my last chance for a really terrific secret, lay it on me," and she spoke about the need to place friendship over love of country, which I must tell you had never crossed my mind one way or the other.

I want to tell you a little bit about my class, the class of 1962. When we came to Wellesley in the fall of 1958, there was an article in the *Harvard Crimson* about the women's colleges, one of those stupid mean little articles full of stereotypes, like girls at Bryn Mawr wear black. We were girls then, by the way, Wellesley girls. How long ago was it? It was so long ago that while I was here, Wellesley actually threw six young women out for lesbianism. It was so long ago that we had curfews. It was so long ago that if you had a boy in your room, you had to leave the door open six inches, and if you closed the door you had to put a sock on the doorknob. In my class of, I don't know, maybe 375 young women, there were six Asians and five blacks. There was a strict quota on the number of Jews. Tuition was $2,000 a year, and in my junior year it was raised to $2,250, and my parents practically had a heart attack.

How long ago? If you needed an abortion, you drove to a gas station in Union, New Jersey, with $500 in cash in an envelope, and you were taken, blindfolded, to a motel room and operated on without an anesthetic. On the lighter side, and as you no doubt read in the *New York Times Magazine*, and were flabbergasted to learn, there were the posture pictures. We not only took off most of our clothes to have our posture pictures taken, we took them off without ever even thinking, "This is weird, why are we doing this?"—not only that, we had also had speech therapy. I was told I had a New Jersey accent I really ought to do something about, which was a shock to me since I was from Beverly Hills, California, and had never set foot in the state of New Jersey . . . not only that, we were required to take a course called Fundamentals, Fundies, where we actually were taught how to get in and out of the back seat of the car. Some of us were named things like Winkie. We all parted our hair in the middle. How long ago was it? It was so long ago that among the things that I honestly cannot conceive of life without, that had not yet been invented: panty hose, lattes, Advil, pasta (there was no pasta then, there was only spaghetti and macaroni)—I sit here writing this speech on a computer next to a touch-tone phone with an answering machine and a Rolodex, there are several CDs on my desk, a bottle of Snapple, there are felt-tip pens and an electric pencil sharpener . . . well, you get the point, it was a long time ago.

Anyway, as I was saying, the *Crimson* had this snippy article which said that Wellesley was a school for Tunicata—Tunicata apparently being small fish who spend the first part of their lives frantically swimming around the ocean floor exploring their environment, and the second part of their lives just lying there breeding. It was mean and snippy, but it had the horrible ring of truth, it was one of those do-not-ask-for-whom-the-bell-tolls things, and it burned itself into our brains. Years later, at my twenty-fifth reunion, one of my classmates mentioned it, and everyone remembered what Tunicata were, word for word.

My class went to college in the era when you got a master's degree in teaching because it was "something to fall back on" in the

LISTEN
HARD

TO WHAT'S GOING ON

and

PLEASE

I BEG YOU,

TAKE IT
PERSONALLY.

worst case scenario, the worst case scenario being that no one married you and you actually had to go to work. As this same classmate said at our reunion, "Our education was a dress rehearsal for a life we never led." Isn't that the saddest line? We weren't meant to have futures; we were meant to marry them. We weren't meant to have politics, or careers that mattered, or opinions, or lives; we were meant to marry them. If you wanted to be an architect, you married an architect. *Non ministrari sed ministrare*—you know the old joke, not to be ministers but to be ministers' wives.

I've written about my years at Wellesley, and I don't want to repeat myself any more than is necessary. But I do want to retell one anecdote from the piece I did about my tenth Wellesley reunion. I'll tell it a little differently for those of you who read it. Which was that, during my junior year, when I was engaged for a very short period of time, I thought I might transfer to Barnard my senior year. I went to see my class dean and she said to me, "Let me give you some advice. You've worked so hard at Wellesley, when you marry, take a year off. Devote yourself to your husband and your marriage." Of course it was a stunning piece of advice to give me because I'd always intended to work after college. My mother was a career woman, and all of us, her four daughters, grew up understanding that the question, "What do you want to be when you grow up?" was as valid for girls as for boys. Take a year off being a wife. I always wondered what I was supposed to do in that year. Iron? I repeated the story for years, as proof that Wellesley wanted its graduates to be merely housewives. But I turned out to be wrong, because years later I met another Wellesley graduate who had been as hell-bent on domesticity as I had been on a career. And she had gone to the same dean with the same problem, and the dean had said to her, "Don't have children right away. Take a year to work." And so I saw that what Wellesley wanted was for us to avoid the extremes. To be instead, that thing in the middle. A lady. We were to take the fabulous education we had received here and use it to preside at dinner table or at a committee meeting, and when two people disagreed we would be intelligent enough to step in and point out the remarkable similarities between their two opposing positions. We were to spend our lives making nice.

Many of my classmates did exactly what they were supposed to when they graduated from Wellesley, and some of them, by the way, lived happily ever after. But many of them didn't. All sorts of things happened that no one expected. They needed money so they had to work. They got divorced so they had to work. They were bored witless so they had to work. The women's movement came along and made harsh value judgments about their lives—judgments that caught them by surprise, because they were doing what they were supposed to be doing, weren't they? The rules had changed; they were caught in some kind of strange time warp. They had never intended to be the heroines of their own lives; they'd intended to be—what?—First Ladies, I guess, first ladies in the lives of big men. They ended up feeling like victims. They ended up, and this is really sad, thinking that their years in college were the best years of their lives.

Why am I telling you this? It was a long time ago, right? Things have changed, haven't they? Yes, they have. But I mention it because I want to remind you of the undertow, of the specific gravity. American society has a remarkable ability to resist change, or to take whatever change has taken place and attempt to make it go away. Things are different for you than they were for us. Just the fact that you chose to come to a single-sex college makes you smarter than we were—we came because it's what you did in those

IN CASE ANY OF YOU
ARE WONDERING,

of course

YOU CAN

HAVE IT ALL.

YOUR EDUCATION IS
A DRESS REHEARSAL

for

A LIFE
THAT IS
YOURS

TO LEAD.

days—and the college you are graduating from is a very different place. All sorts of things caused Wellesley to change, but it did change, and today it's a place that understands its obligations to women in today's world. The women's movement has made a huge difference, too, particularly for young women like you. There are women doctors and women lawyers. There are anchorwomen, although most of them are blonde.

But at the same time, the pay differential between men and women has barely changed. In my business, the movie business, there are many more women directors, but it's just as hard to make a movie about women as it ever was, and look at the parts the Oscar-nominated actresses played this year: hooker, hooker, hooker, hooker, and nun. It's 1996, and you are graduating from Wellesley in the Year of the Wonderbra. The Wonderbra is not a step forward for women. Nothing that hurts that much is a step forward for women.

What I'm saying is, don't delude yourself that the powerful cultural values that wrecked the lives of so many of my classmates have vanished from the earth. Don't let the *New York Times* article about the brilliant success of Wellesley graduates in the business world fool you—there's still a glass ceiling. Don't let the number of women in the work force trick you—there are still lots of magazines devoted almost exclusively to making perfect casseroles and turning various things into tents.

Don't underestimate how much antagonism there is toward women and how many people wish we could turn the clock back. One of the things people always say to you if you get upset is, "Don't take it personally," but listen hard to what's going on and, please, I beg you, take it personally. Understand: Every attack on Hillary Clinton for not knowing her place is an attack on you. Underneath almost all those attacks are the words: get back, get back to where you once belonged. When Elizabeth Dole pretends that she isn't serious about her career, that is an attack on you. The acquittal of O. J. Simpson is an attack on you. Any move to limit abortion rights is an attack on you—whether or not you believe in abortion. The fact that Clarence Thomas is sitting on the Supreme Court today is an attack on you.

Above all, be the heroine of your life, not the victim. Because you don't have the alibi my class had—this is one of the great achievements and mixed blessings you inherit: Unlike us, you can't say nobody told you there were other options. Your education is a dress rehearsal for a life that is yours to lead. Twenty-five years from now, you won't have as easy a time making excuses as my class did. You won't be able to blame the deans, or the culture, or anyone else: You will have no one to blame but yourselves. Whoa.

So what are you going to do? This is the season when a clutch of successful women—who have it all—give speeches to women like you and say: "To be perfectly honest, you can't have it all." Maybe young women don't wonder whether they can have it all any longer, but in case any of you are wondering, of course you can have it all. What are you going to do? Everything, is my guess. It will be a little messy, but embrace the mess. It will be complicated, but rejoice in the complications. It will not be anything like what you think it will be like, but surprises are good for you. And don't be frightened: You can always change your mind. I know: I've had four careers and three husbands.

And this is something else I want to tell you, one of the hundreds of things I didn't know when I was sitting here so many years ago: You are not going to be you, fixed and immutable you, forever. We have a game we play when we're waiting for tables in restaurants,

I hope

YOU WILL FIND SOME WAY TO

BREAK

THE

RULES

AND MAKE A LITTLE TROUBLE

OUT THERE.

where you have to write the five things that describe yourself on a piece of paper. When I was your age, I would have put: ambitious, Wellesley graduate, daughter, Democrat, single. Ten years later not one of those five things turned up on my list. I was: journalist, feminist, New Yorker, divorced, funny. Today not one of those five things turns up in my list: writer, director, mother, sister, happy. Whatever those five things are for you today, they won't make the list in ten years—not that you still won't be some of those things, but they won't be the five most important things about you. Which is one of the most delicious things available to women, and more particularly to women than to men. I think. It's slightly easier for us to shift, to change our minds, to take another path.

Yogi Berra, the former New York Yankee who made a specialty of saying things that were famously maladroit, quoted himself at a recent commencement speech he gave. "When you see a fork in the road," he said, "take it." Yes, it's supposed to be a joke, but as someone said in a movie I made, "Don't laugh, this is my life." This is the life many women lead: Two paths diverge in a wood, and we get to take them both. It's another of the nicest things about being women: We can do that. Did I say it was hard? Yes, but let me say it again so that none of you can ever say the words, "Nobody said it was so hard." But it's also incredibly interesting. You are so lucky to have that life as an option.

Whatever you choose, however many roads you travel, I hope that you choose not to be a lady. I hope you will find some way to break the rules and make a little trouble out there. And I also hope that you will choose to make some of that trouble on behalf of women. Thank you. Good luck. The first act of your life is over. Welcome to the best years of your lives.

····· **NORA EPHRON** ·····

(1941–2012) was a writer, director, and screenwriter
known for creating strong female characters. Her
essay collections *I Feel Bad About My Neck: And
Other Thoughts on Being a Woman* and *I Remember
Nothing* both hit the bestseller list, as did her first
novel, *Heartburn*. She earned Oscar nominations
for her writing on When *Harry Met Sally*, *Silkwood*,
and *Sleepless in Seattle*, and her directorial credits
include the blockbuster films *You've Got Mail* and
Julie & Julia.

Ira Glass

GOUCHER COLLEGE, 2012

I am honored to be asked to be your Commencement speaker. I am still opposed on principle to the idea of a Commencement speech. I believe it is a doomed form, cloying and impossible. Commencement speakers give stock advice, which is then promptly ignored. The central mission of the commencement speech is in itself ridiculous: to inspire at a moment that needs no inspiration.

Look at yourselves at this moment. Something incredible is happening to you, right now. The whole world is opening to you. You guys have been in school your entire lives. You have completed something difficult that took persistence and willfulness. Probably you questioned yourselves, again and again, and now you're off to face the world and do everything that you've been dreaming. What can words add to that, except to delay the moment you get your diploma?

Seriously.

I oppose the form of the Commencement speech, and I continue to oppose it, even as I do one now.

And I said yes only because of my personal connections to this school.

One is your president, Sandy Ungar, whom I worked closely with at NPR years ago. Who, as many of you know, has a special gift for convincing people to do things they do not necessarily want to do. Which worked out great in this case because I have a special gift of saying "yes" to people like that.

Another personal connection I have to Goucher is my Grandma Frieda, my dad's mom, Frieda Friedlander, Goucher Class of '31, a defiantly proud Goucher grad. Are there members of Phi Beta Kappa here? Can I hear? Phi Beta Kappa? You are my grandma's sisters in that organization. I'm wearing her Phi Beta Kappa key right now.

Grandma Frieda wore her key to any special dinner or occasion until she died, and she was not shy about talking about being a member of Phi Beta Kappa with anyone who would listen, which makes her seem like some wacky old-lady crank. She was actually anything but. She was smart and funny and awake to the world. And I loved her enough that, although I oppose the entire tradition of the graduation speech, I am standing here in front of you today because I know it would please her a great deal.

My third connection to Goucher, well, I really was not going to talk about at all. But this week my wife and some friends insisted that you grads would find it relevant. And that is that I lost my virginity in one of the dorms here. Not recently! I was twenty. It was still an all-girls school. I'm not the only one in this tent that has had that experience in one of these dorms, right? She was a Goucher senior. She made this happen; I was not the instigator. I had some good qualities at that age, but I was kind of a little immature and scared. She, however, was used to transcending boundaries, and I think that's all I want to say about that.[1]

Although I oppose the idea of the commencement address, I've been thinking about what would have been useful for me to hear on the day I left college. I wish that someone had said to me that it's normal to feel lost for a little while. You know, you get out of school, you have this great and very expensive education, and you are a rocket ready to launch. It is not clear where you should be pointed, or even how to get off the ground.

And how exactly are you supposed to make this big incredible life that now you're supposedly trained to create? You're supposed to be like, "All right, let's go!" But what do you do?

I think I was as ambitious as any of you in this class. I was working at a network news show, *All Things Considered*, at the age of twenty. And even I floundered. I floundered badly. I had one skill as a person in my twenties, and that is that, for whatever reason, I was a good editor. I was a decent editor from the start. But I knew none of the other things that make me decent at my job now: how to make a story, how to structure a story, how to find a story, how to report. I was a terrible writer. I was the kind of writer who writes a paragraph and then looks at it and thinks, "Oh no! Now I'm going to move all the words around." And then rewrites it over and over again.

I spent years in my twenties doing mediocre stories that should have taken days but, in fact, took me months. I spent years wondering if I should just learn to become a journalist by going to journalism school, by going to grad school. Instead—and this is just a little practical tip—I simply decided to take NPR reporters and pay them $50 to look at scripts I was working on, which was much cheaper than grad school.

My parents, throughout my twenties when I was working in public radio, completely opposed everything that I was doing working in public broadcasting. Somehow my parents are the only Jews in America who do not listen to public radio. They thought I should be a doctor. I was once a pre-med student, among other things. Their idea for my life was that I'd have some kids and live here in the Baltimore suburbs where I grew up, like their parents' kids. I hope this is not embarrassing to them if I say this: I had my own national radio show, I had been on David Letterman, and there had been a *New York Times Magazine* article about me before they stopped suggesting medical school was still an option.

And to their great credit, they changed. I think one of the most difficult things for any parent is to re-align his or her expectations for their kids with what their kids actually want to be.

And I think when you're the kid in that situation, it's really easy to be glib and just expect your parents to drop their preconceptions and catch up instantly to your idea of who you want to be.

In my case, my parents were worried about money. They both grew up without much money, financially insecure. They saw that I was making no money doing public broadcasting, and it just pushed all of their buttons. They were really worried. When I was in my twenties, things were said between us that, well, my mom passed away a few years ago of cancer, and there are things I said to her in my twenties that I still regret.

I think my parents adjusted their ideas for what my life should be with as much grace as anybody could. And I would just say to you guys, as your parents struggle with that supremely difficult task: Don't be a dick.

There's a show on HBO that I admire a lot, called *Girls*. It's about what it's like in the years after college when you're trying to make a life for yourself. It's about what you guys are about to launch yourselves into. Every single fact about that show is completely

IT'S NORMAL TO FEEL LOST

FOR A LITTLE WHILE.

different from my life when I was in my twenties, but the essence of that show feels exactly the same. What's great about the show is that it's a completely unromantic view of what your life is about to become. The young women on that show, they flounder, they pretend to know what they're doing when they absolutely don't. They strongly believe things that are transparently untrue. I myself spent years—*years!*—in a terrible kind of politically correct phase where I traveled to Nicaragua—and called it "Neekah-rahg-you-ah"—to observe the Sandinista revolution firsthand.

You will be stupid. You will worry your parents as I worried mine. You will question your own choices. You will question your relationships, your jobs, your friends, where you live, what you studied in college, that you went to college at all, and the thing I want to say is: That is totally okay. That is totally normal. If that happens, you're doing it right.

When you're in school you're on a path, and there are signposts, and there are goals. They give you grades, which, in retrospect, is an insanely wonderful thing that people are constantly grading you and telling you, "You did well!" "You did badly!" "You did well!"

Now you are going to join the confusing mess of life with me and your parents and the rest of us, the mess that we've been living inside for years ahead of you, where it is not clear at all how to evaluate anything that you are doing or how you're going to spend the rest of this time on this earth.

Welcome to your future.

The good news is that you can will things into existence. Like, I was not a very good writer, and I just willed it to happen by trying and trying and trying.

You leave this school as well-armed for battle as anyone is. You're doing as well as anybody. And now you'll just have to invent

The

GOOD NEWS
IS THAT

YOU CAN
WILL
THINGS

into

EXISTENCE.

what you're going to be. That's what I did. I would work and work and work and make up little series that I'd produce on *Morning Edition*, and I just assumed that ideas would be sprinkled on me like fairy dust: You wake up, and you have a good idea. I had to learn that finding an idea is a job. If you're going to do creative work, you have to invent a system to find ideas to make the work *about*. That is a job in itself.

Finding an idea is a job.

And where do ideas come from? They come from other ideas. And you have to surround yourself with things that are interesting to you and notice what's exciting to you and what you want to dive into. Finding what you're going to make your short story or film or song or art project about is a job. Finding what you want to do next is a job. It's a task. You have to set aside hours in the day, and you have to be a soldier, and you have to fight for what you're going to make yourself into.

You cannot tell where things will lead. My Grandma Frieda, after she got out of Goucher, her life took some really, really rough turns. She graduated in 1931 during a slight economic turndown you might have heard of. She divorced soon after having two children. She was a single mom during the Depression and afterward.

Back when she was a teenager here in Baltimore, to treat her acne (she had bad acne), they had this brand-new, amazing technology called X-rays. They would expose your skin to it in high doses to clear up your zits. Only later did they realize that high doses of radiation like that give you skin cancer, which kicked in for Grandma Frieda when she was thirty-two. They had to remove most of the skin from her face and graft on skin from elsewhere on her body, which took over forty separate operations.

She was the first one on either side of my family to have gone to college but ended up taking over the family business, which was a little corner grocery down on Bayard Street downtown—basically a Jewish bodega—that the family lived upstairs from, where my dad and my uncle also worked.

She talked about Goucher so fondly as she got older because, I think, she was happy here. It was a really happy time in her life. My dad and my uncle both told me this week that after Goucher, things got a lot harder for her.

Eventually, she did the job she trained for at Goucher, which was to be a teacher.

In her files here at Goucher there are evaluations from teaching classes that she took. There's one dated April 1931: "Miss Fried-lander gives promise of being a very successful teacher. She has a sense of social responsibility, a pleasing personality, an excellent and well-trained mind." Her teaching practice met "great success, making unusual, varied, interesting, well-organized lesson plans, presenting her material with force and vigor . . . clinching her points in a most experienced manner."

Eventually, she taught French in the public high schools here in Baltimore, in the city, at a high school that confusingly is called City College. Apparently she was very good at it. A writer named Dwayne Wickham wrote a memoir about growing up in Baltimore and struggling in school and nearly dropping out, and he names her as one of the few teachers who tried to rescue him as he struggled through high school. Just as her teachers at Goucher predicted.

I'm going to close with a story that seems crazy, but I remember her telling this story, and my dad insists it's true. It's about the day that Grandma Frieda, Goucher grad, Bawlmer girl, met Adolf Hitler. She was married in June 1932, and there was enough money from the corner store at that point to honeymoon in Europe, in Germany. She and my grandfather, Louie, were getting a tour of some government building. I was always told that it was the Reichstag building, which burned down a year later. They were led through a room—you know you get in with a group of tourists and are led through various rooms?—they walk into a room, and the tour guide says, "Oh, this is Herr Hitler, you know, who's trying to become our new chancellor."

My Grandma Frieda would later describe him as this short, unimpressive little man.

And he nods at the foreign tourists, and they kinda nod at him and move on to the next room.

Years later, in her high school classroom at City College, my Grandma Frieda would tell this story, and she said the response was always the same from the students. They would always say the same thing. They would raise their hands and go, "Why didn't you kill him?"

And she'd said, "Well, if I'd have KNOWN what he was going to DO! It was 1932!"

And right there is the problem. We don't know. We lurch forward in our lives. We try this. We try that. We make the best guesses that we can, based on what we believe at the time. And it is entirely possible that a Goucher grad—that you, or you, or you—will get the chance to change the world and kill Adolf Hitler. And you will miss it.

That is entirely possible.

But I have to say, I talked to a lot of you last night, and I believe in you.

I think that it is just as likely that you will continue to grow and build muscle, which is your next task, and continue to make yourselves into who it is you are trying to be. And when you get your chance to remake the world, when you get the chance to change everything for yourself, and hopefully for others, too, when you get your chance to shoot Adolf Hitler, you will know what to do.

That's my wish for you on this day.

1. "Transcending boundaries" was a Goucher slogan and catchphrase that year.

····· **IRA GLASS** ·····
is the host of WBEZ Chicago's
This American Life.

Barbara Kingsolver

L et me begin this way: with an invocation of your own best hopes, thrown like a handful of rice over this celebration. Congratulations, graduates. Congratulations, parents, on the best Mother's Day gift ever. Better than all those burnt-toast breakfasts: these, your children grown tall and competent, educated to within an inch of their lives.

What can I say to people who know almost everything? There was a time when I surely knew, because I'd just graduated from college myself, after writing down the sum of all human knowledge on exams and research papers. But that great pedagogical swilling-out must have depleted my reserves, because decades have passed and now I can't believe how much I don't know. Looking back, I can discern a kind of gaseous exchange in which I exuded cleverness and gradually absorbed better judgment. Wisdom is like frequent-flyer miles and scar tissue: If it does accumulate, that happens by accident while you're trying to do something else. And wisdom is what people will start wanting from you, after your last exam. I know it's true for writers—when people love a book, whatever they say about it, what they really mean is: It was *wise*. It helped explain their pickle. My favorites are the canny old codgers: Neruda, García Márquez, Doris Lessing. Honestly, it is harrowing for me to try to teach twenty-year-old students who earnestly want to improve their writing. The best I can think to tell them is: quit smoking, and observe posted speed limits. This will improve your odds of getting old enough to be wise.

The world shifts under our feet. The rules change.

If I stopped there, you might have heard my best offer. But I am charged with postponing your diploma for about fifteen more minutes, so I'll proceed, with a caveat. The wisdom of each generation is necessarily new. This tends to dawn on us in revelatory moments, brought to us by our children. For example: My younger daughter is eleven. Every morning, she and I walk down the lane from our farm to the place where she meets the school bus. It's the best part of my day. We have great conversations. But a few weeks ago as we stood waiting in the dawn's early light, Lily was quietly looking me over, and finally said: "Mom, just so you know, the only reason I'm letting you wear that outfit is because of your age." The *alleged outfit* will not be described here; whatever you're imagining will perfectly suffice. (Especially if you're picturing *Project Runway* meets "working with livestock.") Now, I believe parents should uphold respect for adult authority, so I did what I had to do. I hid behind the barn when the bus came.

And then I walked back up the lane in my fly regalia, contemplating this new equation: "because of your age." It's okay now to deck out and turn up as the village idiot. Hooray! I am old enough. How does this happen? Over a certain age, do you become invisible? There is considerable evidence for this in movies and television. But mainly, I think, you're not expected to know the rules. Everyone knows you're operating on software that hasn't been updated for a good while.

The world shifts under our feet. The rules change. Not the Bill of Rights, or the rules of tenting, but the big unspoken truths of a generation. Exhaled by culture, taken in like oxygen, we hold these truths to be self-evident: You get what you pay for. Success is everything. Work is what you do for money, and that's what counts. How could it be otherwise? And the converse of that last rule, of course, is that if you're not paid to do a thing, it can't be important. If a child writes a poem and proudly reads it, adults may wink and ask, "Think there's a lot of money in that?" You may also hear this when you declare a major in English. Being a good neighbor, raising children: The road to success is not paved with the likes of these. Some workplaces actually quantify your likelihood of being distracted by family or volunteerism. It's called your Coefficient of Drag. The ideal number is zero. This is the Rule of Perfect Efficiency.

Now, the rule of "Success" has traditionally meant having boatloads of money. But we are not really supposed to put it in a boat. A house would be the customary thing. Ideally it should be large, with a lot of bathrooms and so forth, but no more than four people. If two friends come over during approved visiting hours, the two children have to leave. The bathroom-to-resident ratio should at all times remain greater than one. I'm not making this up, I'm just observing; it's more or less my profession. As Yogi Berra told us, you can observe a lot just by watching. I see our dream houses standing alone, the idealized life taking place in a kind of bubble. So you need another bubble, with rubber tires, to convey yourself to places you must visit, such as an office. If you're successful, it will be a large, empty-ish office you don't have to share. If you need anything, you can get it delivered. Play your cards right and you may never have to come face to face with another person. This is the Rule of Escalating Isolation.

And so we find ourselves in the chapter of history I would entitle "Isolation and Efficiency, And How They Came Around to Bite Us in the Backside." Because it's looking that way. We're a world at war, ravaged by disagreements, a bizarrely globalized people in which the extravagant excesses of one culture wash up as famine or flood on the shores of another. Even the architecture of our planet is collapsing under the weight of our efficient productivity. Our climate, our oceans, migratory paths, things we believed were independent of human affairs. Twenty years ago, climate scientists first told Congress that unlimited carbon emissions were building toward a disastrous instability. Congress said, "We need to think about that." About ten years later, nations of the world wrote the Kyoto Protocol, a set of legally binding controls on our carbon emissions. The U.S. said, "We still need to think about it." Now we can watch as glaciers disappear, the lights of biodiversity go out, the oceans reverse their ancient orders. A few degrees looked so small on the thermometer. We are so good at measuring things and declaring them under control. How could our weather turn murderous, pummel our coasts, and push new diseases like dengue fever onto our doorsteps? It's an emergency on a scale we've never known. We've responded by following the rules we know: Efficiency, Isolation. We can't slow down our productivity and consumption; that's unthinkable. Can't we just go home and put a really big lock on the door?

Not this time. Our paradigm has met its match. The world will save itself, don't get me wrong. The term "fossil fuels" is not a metaphor or a simile. In the geological sense, it's over. The internal combustion engine is so twentieth century. Now we can either shift away from a carbon-based economy or find another place to live. Imagine it: We raised you on a lie. Everything you plug in, turn on, or drive, the out-of-season foods you eat, the music in your ears. We gave you this world and promised you could keep it running on: *a fossil substance*. Dinosaur slime, and it's running out. The geologists only disagree on how much is left, and the climate scientists are now saying they're sorry but that's not even the point. We won't get time to use it all. To stabilize the floods and firestorms, we'll have to reduce our carbon emissions by 80 percent, within a decade.

"YOU CAN OBSERVE A LOT JUST BY WATCHING."

Heaven help us get our minds around that. We're still stuck on a strategy of bait and switch: OK, we'll keep the cars, but run them on ethanol made from corn! But—we use petroleum to grow the corn. Even if you like the idea of robbing the food bank to fill up the tank, there is a math problem: It takes nearly a gallon of fossil

YOU DON'T NEED SO MUCH STUFF

TO FILL YOUR LIFE
WHEN YOU HAVE PEOPLE IN IT.

fuel to render an equivalent gallon of corn gas. By some accounts, it takes more. Think of the Jules Verne novel in which the hero is racing Around the World in Eighty Days, and finds himself stranded in the mid-Atlantic on a steamship that's run out of coal. It's Day Seventy-Nine. So Phileas Fogg convinces the Captain to pull up the decks and throw them into the boiler. "On the next day the masts, rafts, and spars were burned. The crew worked lustily, keeping up the fires. There was a perfect rage for demolition." The Captain remarked, "Fogg, you've got something of the Yankee about you." Oh, novelists. They always manage to have the last word, even when they are dead.

How can we get from here to there, without burning up our ship? That will be central question of your adult life: to escape the wild rumpus of carbon-fuel dependency, in the nick of time. You'll make rules that were previously unthinkable, imposing limits on what we can use and possess. You will radically reconsider the power relationship between humans and our habitat. In the words of my esteemed colleague and friend Wendell Berry, the new Emancipation Proclamation will not be for a specific race or species, but for life itself. Imagine it. Nations have already joined together to rein in global consumption. Faith communities have found a new point of agreement with student activists, organizing around the conviction that caring for our planet is a moral obligation. Before the last U.N. Climate Conference, in Bali, thousands of U.S. citizens contacted the State Department to press for binding limits on carbon emissions. We're the 5 percent of humans who have made 50 percent of all the greenhouse gases up there. But our government is reluctant to address it, for one reason: It might hurt our economy.

For a lot of history, many nations said exactly the same thing about abolishing slavery. We can't grant humanity to all people: It would hurt our cotton plantations, our sugar crop, our balance of trade. Until the daughters and sons of a new wisdom declared: We don't care. You have to find another way. Enough of this shame.

Have we lost that kind of courage? Have we let economic growth become our undisputed master again? As we track the unfolding disruption of natural and global stabilities, you will be told to buy into business as usual: You need a job. Trade your future for an entry level position. Do what we did, preserve a profitable climate for manufacture and consumption, at any cost. Even at the cost of the other climate—the one that was hospitable to life as we knew it. Is anyone thinking this through? In the awful moment when someone demands at gunpoint, "Your money or your life," that's not supposed to be a hard question.

Generosity is not out of the question.

A lot of people, in fact, are rethinking the money answer. Looking behind the cash price of everything, to see what it cost us elsewhere: to mine and manufacture, to transport, to burn, to bury. What did it harm on its way here? Could I get it closer to home? Previous generations rarely asked about the hidden costs. We put them on layaway. You don't get to do that. The bill has come due. Some European countries already are calculating the "climate cost" on consumer goods and adding it to the price. The future is here. We're examining the moralities of possession, inventing renewable technologies, recovering sustainable food systems. We're even

The

HARDEST PART
WILL BE TO

CONVINCE
YOURSELF

of the

POSSIBILITIES,

and

HANG ON.

YOU CAN BE AS

EARNEST

and

RIDICULOUS

AS YOU NEED TO BE,

if you

DON'T ATTEMPT IT
IN ISOLATION.

warming up to the idea that the wealthy nations will have to help the poorer ones, for the sake of a reconstructed world. We've done it before. That was the Marshall Plan. Generosity is not out of the question. It will grind some gears in the machine of Efficiency. But we can retool.

We can also rethink the big, lonely house as a metaphor for success. You are in a perfect position to do that. You've probably spent very little of your recent life in a free-standing unit with a bathroom-to-resident ratio of greater than one. (Maybe more like 1:200.) You've been living so close to your friends, you didn't have to ask about their problems, you had to step over them to get into the room. As you moved from dormitory to apartment to whatever you've had such a full life, surrounded by people, in all kinds of social and physical structures, none of which belonged entirely to you. You're told that's all about to change. That growing up means leaving the herd, starting up the long escalator to isolation.

Not necessarily. As you leave here, remember what you loved most in this place. Not Orgo 2, I'm guessing, or the crazed squirrels or even the bulk cereal in the Freshman Marketplace. I mean the way you lived, in close and continuous contact. This is an ancient human social construct that once was common in this land. We called it a community. We lived among our villagers, depending on them for what we needed. If we had a problem, we did not discuss it over the phone with someone in Bhubaneshwar. We went to a neighbor. We acquired food from farmers. We listened to music in groups, in churches or on front porches. We danced. We participated. Even when there was no money in it. Community is our native state. You play hardest for a hometown crowd: You become your best self. You know joy. This is not a guess; there is evidence.

The scholars who study social well-being can put it on charts and graphs. In the last thirty years our material wealth has increased in this country, but our self-described happiness has steadily declined. Elsewhere, the people who consider themselves very happy are not in the very poorest nations, as you might guess, nor in the very richest. The winners are Mexico, Ireland, Puerto Rico, the kinds of places we identify with extended family, noisy villages, a lot of dancing. The happiest people are the ones with the most community.

YOU'LL SEE THINGS COLLAPSE IN YOUR TIME, THE BIG HOUSES, THE EMPIRES OF GLASS. THE NEW GREEN THINGS THAT SPROUT UP THROUGH THE WRECK— THOSE WILL BE YOURS.

You can take that to the bank. I'm not sure what they'll do with it down there, but you could try. You could walk out of here with an unconventionally communal sense of how your life may be. This could be your key to a new order: You don't need so much stuff to fill your life when you have people in it. You don't need jet fuel to get food from a farmer's market. You could invent a new kind of Success that includes children's poetry, butterfly migrations, butterfly kisses, the Grand Canyon, eternity. If somebody says, "Your money or your life," you could say: life. And mean it. You'll see things collapse in your time, the big houses, the empires of glass. The new green things that sprout up through the wreck—those will be yours.

The arc of history is longer than human vision. It bends. We abolished slavery, we granted universal suffrage. We have done hard things before. And every time it took a terrible fight between people who could not imagine changing the rules and those who said, "We already did. We have made the world new." The hardest part will be to convince yourself of the possibilities, and hang on. If you run out of hope at the end of the day, to rise in the morning and put it on again with your shoes. Hope is the only reason you won't give in, burn what's left of the ship, and go down with it. The ship of your natural life and your children's only shot. You have to love that so earnestly—you, who were born into the Age of Irony. Imagine getting caught with your Optimism hanging out. It feels so risky. Like showing up at the bus stop as the village idiot. You may be asked to stand behind the barn. You may feel you're not up to the task.

But think of this: What if someone had dared you, three years ago, to show up to some public event wearing a big, flappy dress with sleeves down to your knees? And on your head, oh, let's say, a beanie with a square board on top. And a tassel! Look at you. You are beautiful. The magic is community. The time has come for the square beanie, and you are rocked in the bosom of the people who get what you're going for. You can be as earnest and ridiculous as you need to be, if you don't attempt it in isolation. The ridiculously earnest are known to travel in groups. And they are known to change the world. Look at you. That could be you.

I'll close with a poem:

Hope, An Owner's Manual

Look, you might as well know, this thing
is going to take endless repair: rubber bands,
crazy glue, tapioca, the square of the hypotenuse.
Nineteenth-century novels. Heartstrings, sunrise:
all of these are useful. Also, feathers.

To keep it humming, sometimes you have to stand
on an incline, where everything looks possible,
on the line you drew yourself. Or in
the grocery line, making faces at a toddler
secretly, over his mother's shoulder.

You might have to pop the clutch and run
past all the evidence. Past everyone who is
laughing or praying for you. Definitely you don't
want to go directly to jail, but still, here you go,
passing time, passing strange. Don't pass this up.

In the worst of times, you will have to pass it off.
Park it and fly by the seat of your pants. With nothing
in the bank, you'll still want to take the express.
Tiptoe past the dogs of the apocalypse that are sleeping
in the shade of your future. Pay at the window.
Pass your hope like a bad check.
You might still have just enough time. To make a deposit.

Congratulations, graduates.

····· **BARBARA KINGSOLVER** ·····

is an internationally acclaimed American author.
Her novel *The Poisonwood Bible* was a Pulitzer
Prize finalist and an Oprah's Book Club selection,
and *The Lacuna* received Britain's Orange Prize for
Fiction. In 2011, she earned the prestigious Dayton
Literary Peace Prize for lifetime achievement.
In 1999, Kingsolver created the Bellwether Prize for
Fiction, a biennial award honoring first-time novelists
for literature that fosters social justice.
She lives in southwestern Virginia.

Eileen Myles

HAMPSHIRE COLLEGE, 1998

I was wondering if all commencement speakers feel compelled to address their own college experience. I'd rather not. I wanted to focus on you guys, even just for a little while; I tried to get some statistics from the school about who you are—you know, boys and girls, straight and gay, racially, ethnically, economically, and age-wise. I bet you're not all twenty-one years old, but here it is May 16 and I never found out. You have these outfits on, but that's all that's the same. One by one you know who you are. I bet a few of you are depressed. Not everyone feels good at graduation. Some of you feel great, some of you are worried, someone's sick, someone's in love, someone's mother died this year. Maybe not. I hope that's not true, but it happens. Everything does. I have some photographs of myself graduating from college, I didn't bring them, but those pictures replaced any memories I might have had of that day. I see me from the outside walking down an aisle in a white cap and gown in Boston and that's all that I know. I'd like to be here with you.

You have given me an honorable job. I didn't know what I was going to do with my life when I got out of college. I'm forty-eight; I'm probably a lot of your parents' age, more or less. I haven't had any kids; I mean I definitely won't. It's a very hot year, 1998, the earth moving closer and closer to the sun and me going through menopause, so I probably wasn't going to have any kids anyhow, but now I definitely won't, but I teach a lot, and I have a lot of friends in their twenties, and I like your generation a lot. I feel very close to you, and you'd probably like my poetry if you read it, it's basically just like this talk, it's something to do. Being a poet is a job, but it's a made-up one. There's no job description, and that's what I like. I liked the vague feeling of being in college; it may not have been that way for you, well, it wasn't for me. It was exciting, I discovered that loving literature could be a job, and then I decided I didn't want that one, and I got depressed, and a lot more happened to me when I was in college, but what was wonderful about college as an institution is that it encompassed that—everything that I felt, it held me for a while, and people would say, what do you do? and I'd say that I was a student and they'd say great. You couldn't go wrong, it was like washing your clothes. No one argues with laundry, or the identity of a student; it's a cyclical thing you just have to go through, and I did.

I mean it's a little like riding a bike. You just keep pedaling, and the wheels go round and round and you get someplace. You can't help it. And you see someone you know and they say, what are you doing? and you say, riding a bike. I mean you could have just robbed a bank, but it looks so innocent.

This is a nice place. It must have been nice to go to school here. It's a beautiful place. The thing I found about being outside of college is that you have to figure out when everything stops and starts. You walk into the bank and you get in line. You may not like it, but you stay. You don't have to. You go into a restaurant and you get a cup of coffee and the coffee's bad and you get up and walk out. You go home and you call a friend. Then you think, I wish I called someone else. One day you're standing in front of the Eiffel Tower and you think, this is great. It is exactly the way I expected it. I had that feeling at least once in my life. Some things are utterly satisfying. The Taj Mahal, on the other hand, was a total disappointment. India was not. But the Taj Mahal was not so good. Life is so incomplete. College isn't. It isn't at all. It's just you.

The thing I found about being outside of college is that you have to figure out when everything stops and starts.

So I just got out of college and I've done an awful lot of things, but basically I started traveling and writing poems. I like traveling because I like an activity, but you really don't know what you're going to get. Russia, for instance, just kind of ruined my life. I didn't know that was going to happen. How would I know that? I wanted to change my life. Now I've got to wait a few years to see exactly in what way it ruined my life so I can write about it. Basically, I've

WHATEVER'S
NEXT TO EACH OTHER
COUNTS

ASSEMBLAGE
MAKES THE
TRUTH

been writing poems. I got out of college and they just came pouring out of me. They're all over everything. Napkins, stationery from so many different jobs. Notebooks, notebooks of all sizes.

Actually I was looking at a big box of notebooks the other day, and I pulled one out of the box, 1964. I was fourteen. In the notebook I would talk about school, and I would talk about what I ate, and how Janet felt about me, but there was this one thing: It would go March 5th: C+ day. Then it would be a not bad day: B minus. I was rating the days, that's what my life was when I was fourteen. I couldn't imagine living without saying how much. How bad, how good. That's what I did. I looked around. I had stopped praying by then. But I looked at time, rows of it, days and days, the ones I was in and I said bad, good, okay.

But I don't do that anymore. See, a poem is a tiny institution. I just write lots and lots of them, and it gives me a way to be in the world. It's actually a very worldly job; there really isn't a wrong place to be, a poet kind of goes with anything, any kind of decor, indoor, out. Presidents like to have poets next to them, we're sort of like a speaking wreath, the kind of poet you pick tells the kind of president you are. The hell of dating or marrying a poet is that certainly we will write about you, so if you don't want to be seen, don't date a poet, anyone should know that. Because really, a poet has nothing better to do than look at you. A poet's best friend is her dog, because instantly the dog will take the poet on walks; the poet is like the earth's shadow. The sun moves and the poet writes something down. I felt so happy to be invited here by the class of '98 that I bought a new suit. I guess by now you've gotten the idea that I am your poet. So I feel good, and I look good, and now I'd like to go a little further, simply doing my job.

The notion of leadership changes every few years. Right now

we like to have a leader that we don't mind looking at, whose antics we may not approve of, but we know about. We like to know everything we can about our leaders today. We don't care much about their private lives. We're excited by a leader who likes to live publicly. I think we're living in a public moment and that's why poets need to come back. While we're all living on the outside we need someone living on the inside, to watch themselves and then us, to bring our inside out. Do you know what I mean? Our time needs a shadow. We know this, but we have to hear it too. I'll tell you about the history of this.

WHILE WE'RE ALL LIVING ON THE OUTSIDE WE NEED SOMEONE LIVING ON THE INSIDE, TO WATCH THEMSELVES AND THEN US, TO BRING OUR INSIDE OUT.

About 300 years ago there was a poet in New Spain, which is what they called Mexico then, and her name was Sor Juana Inés de la Cruz. I'm sure some of you have read her, have heard about her. The man who was her biographer, Octavio Paz, died just a couple of months ago. Anyway, she was indeed the first poet of North America, even before Anne Bradstreet, and she was world famous—a big library at that time in the world would have about 400 volumes, and in that library would be her books; everyone in the world who read, read Sor Juana Inéz de la Cruz.

Now, this is a poet who did not travel. In fact she didn't even go out. Her work did, of course. She lived inside a convent in Mexico City and because she was friends with a great many powerful people in the church and the government, she would be invited to write the important poems commemorating the events of her time. To do that public thing.

I bought a refrigerator the other day, the first refrigerator I have ever bought in my life, and the man in the store, Gringer's on First Avenue, asked me what I do, and I said I'm a poet. "Let's hear one," he said. I balked, maybe feeling a little cheesy, you know like I should entertain him while I'm buying a refrigerator, like those cab drivers or waiters who flirt with women while they work, so that you're reminded that you're never really a customer, you're always just a woman, or a poet. I recited one—not well—I kind of stuttered. It was short. He looked at me blankly. "Do you want to hear it again?" I asked. No. "I think that one went over my head," he said, and turned his attention to the next customer.

When a new Viceroy, a new leader, arrived in New Spain, the local government would commission a ceremonial arch, and the Viceroy and his wife would pass under it with much fanfare. Think about that when you look at arches, that they describe important moments, that someone commissioned someone else to make them, that supposedly an arch celebrates an important moment, that someone passes through. The greatest sculptor would design the arch, usually with images of Poseidon, and cherubim, and vanquished Indians, and beautiful women, whatever was chic, and the poet would write a poem to be read as the procession of glorious new people would walk under, going from this moment to that; it's a history you can see, like what we're doing today.

Most poets teach, I do, and school just ended everywhere in the world, and towards the end of the semester, I find myself getting continually more kind of woo-woo and risky, wanting to go out into the world with my writing class; mostly I've already told them everything I know, and I want to have an experience together, so we went to see some art, we took a trip up to 112th Street, to St. John the Divine. Inside one of the small chapels that line the cathedral walls there's an installation by the video artist Bill Viola. It's a triptych, and though the contents of his piece are extremely obvious, they really work. The first panel is a woman giving birth. A youngish, maybe early thirties, white woman who is cradled between her husband's open legs. It looks like the ideal birth—both of the people are calm and beautiful and there are midwives hovering, and the tape is clearly edited, but we get the whole experience. The infant's head is pushing out from between the beautiful, suffering young woman's legs.

The middle triptych is a man floating under water. It might be Bill Viola; he's wearing a flowing robe and there's a wire that he's dangled on, and the robe is rippling, and it might be anyone, some lonely baby in the middle of his life—hopelessly connected and submerged in "it," whatever the substance is, and clearly alone.

The final panel is an old woman on a life-support system, and she finally dies. Turns out it's Bill Viola's mother. The entire installation cycle lasts thirty minutes. I found myself sobbing at the moment of the birth. It was so riveting, I knew I was going to do it; I've been crying all over the place lately, and this was such a good cry, the cry of birth.

Later we sat in a little garden outside the cathedral. It was a class, after all, and isn't this the definition of academy—a grove of trees? We sat around another sculpture, a big sunflower, and we

I'M
HAPPY
TO BE ALIVE
WITH
YOU

talked about Bill Viola and the Walter Benjamin essay I had asked them to read for today, and it was really perfect, because the essay was "The Work of Art in the Age of Mechanical Reproduction," and here we have birth and videotape in a church. All of us were enjoying each other's intelligence and the nice weather, and then a beautiful peacock stepped into our midst, a real one, and it sprayed open its feathers, hundreds of eyes like old TV. I told them, "NBC," and then we got on the train downtown.

This is greatness,
to pass through and
know, to know that
it's happening to you,
to be awake at the
moment of birth.

I rode downtown with two students, Allison and Tanya, and they told me about the altar of the church, which I hadn't looked at, and how there was a great man for each century, and the spot for the twentieth century was empty, and also it was the final century, so how could that spot be filled, it was so ominous. We had a moment of silence for the twentieth century. I suggested Gandhi; Gandhi's great, we agreed. But if the twentieth century is the final spot on the altar, shouldn't it just be the gateway to all other centuries, not just the last? And what great person could do that? We couldn't think of any great women—great in the right way. There's Mother Teresa and Gertrude Stein; we discussed the scandals in both of their lives. I suggested the woman giving birth. It's just a great act, that great act makes all the other ones possible; it's an act of allowing, of not destroying, of giving, letting life pass through, and I thought I should bring this to you. What a frightening thought, a woman's body being the archway to the future, and as we stand here, and some of you will be giving birth, or being there and holding her, and some of you have already done this, and here are your kids, they sit in their seats today, graduating from college. This is greatness, to pass through and know, to know that it's happening to you, to be awake at the moment of birth.

A friend of mine, Susie, is a death-penalty lawyer. I guess I should be frank with you. You may or may not have been obsessed with graduating from college this spring. But I have. When you invite a poet, you are inviting someone who is obsessed, who has nothing better to do, who wants to be your arch. I do weddings and funerals. In 1992 I ran for president. It was the right thing to do with that year. So all spring while you have been thinking about graduation, or not at all, I've been gathering things for you. I wondered who you were. I saw the moment of birth at the cathedral, and I thought that would be great for the class of '98.

I was in Hawaii this spring; I was invited there to do a reading and a talk, and I was taken for walks in the national park, and I saw the form of worship they have there. You will see in holy places in Hawaii a pile of rocks, it's called a *heiau*, and it simply notates a holy place, three or four rocks, sometimes a flower and a toy, a can of pop, and no one disturbs these piles, it's a site of worship. I was giving a talk at the University of Hawaii, it was called "How to Write a Poem," and I guess in my illustration, I was unwittingly doing the same thing, telling them that the poem could just be a pile of things, for instance—and I grabbed a young man's can of juice—I mean, I asked—I said, could I have this for a moment? He said sure, and I said that the poem could be like red chair, can of Hawaiian Punch, man's leg—that whatever's next to each other counts, the assemblage makes the truth, the truth of the poem. I met that young man later at a reading and he told me that he liked my talk very much, but there was one problem. "You never gave me my juice back." I looked at him. "I was thirsty," he said.

All spring I've been gathering the most important things I can think of and putting them together. When I was a child I would take these long walks, before I could write, before I had language, and I would come home and my mother would say, empty your pockets. And there was my poem: a piece of bright glass, a stone. A little piece of wood.

Susie is a death-penalty lawyer, and when I told her I was coming to talk at your graduation, she said I think this would be interesting to you. We went to the Supreme Court in Brooklyn last week. We are all sitting in our seats. Here's the courtroom. Over there is the jury. A few white people, mostly black and Hispanic, the courtroom is so small. Susie said, that's bad. The jury is right on top of the prosecution. The DA is a woman named Heidi; she looked familiar, we made eye contact right away. She's very smart, the judge is female, white. I don't know what happened to her, says Susie. She has no patience, watch her. Our client is going to fry, if she has her way. I'm sitting on the left. I'm sitting with Susie and the defense. Again, we're all white. On the left side of the courtroom, I mean the audience side, is the family, the relatives, mother, brothers of the people who died, the massacred, the victims, the slain.

Here's the story. Darryl Harris, a young African-American man, the one sitting right in front of us in the courtroom, he worked at Rikers Island, a New York City prison, for many years. He was a hero; he saved at least one man's life in a prison riot and was decorated by the City of New York. He began to smoke crack cocaine, and eventually he lost his job and then worked as a security guard for a while, and lost that job too from smoking dope, and one night last year he was hanging out in a social club, Club Happiness, in Brooklyn. Darryl Harris flipped. No one denies that. He shot four men he knew in the back of their heads. He made them lie down.

The young DA in the green suit questions the detective who came to the scene of the crime that December morning and counted the bodies and helped create an overhead drawing, a diagram of the social club, and the DA questions him. Did you see a pack of Newports on the bar? Yes. Can you point to that place on the drawing? Did you see a white baseball cap? Yes. One woman was slain. She watched the deaths of all the others; she begged for her life. She had five children, and he chased her, there was a struggle, he repeatedly stabbed her, and her body was found outside by the detective. He was directed to her body by a homeless man; she was lying on an abandoned mattress outside the club. Is this photograph accurate, the DA asked. Yes. And later you identified her in the morgue.

It is so emotional, the courtroom scene. Clearly we are being brought through this scene step-by-step so we will feel horror, slow creeping horror, of how one of us can, has, Darryl Harris has eradicated five other people's lives, and here are their families to my left, and there is the jury peering around, guilty themselves, there is the judge in her white hair. Often the defense and the judge and the prosecution have to get up and go into the judge's chambers and say something that the jury can't hear, and Darryl Harris sits there alone at a long table and he's wearing a green sweater, and he's a handsome man, he looks sweet. I kind of want to touch his head and forgive him, because the horror of all this is that everything has happened already, every horrible thing has happened already, that is the truth and now we have to decide whether we should destroy Darryl Harris, who lost his mind one night, and though he is a man in a green sweater, with a teeny gold earring in his ear, looking strong, looking vulnerable, murderer, even looking sad, laughing softly for a moment with his lawyer, clearly we should put him down. He did something incredibly wrong, and this courtroom scene is tense, is a frozen greasy portrait of his life, probably the end of it. But the drawing was the most emotional scene, oddly. It all came true, when they pinned it to the wall. When we had a plan, a layout. The man I spoke to in the hall agreed. He's a *New Yorker* writer. Do you come to a lot of these? No, he smiles. It's an important case. It's amazing, he agrees. It quickens it. Not exactly art, but an order. It says we must be here.

Where are we now? I don't want that man to die. Do you? It made me want to be a lawyer. I thought I've done everything wrong, I want to go back, to go to law school, to take part in this rite of confusion and justice and race and narrative and drugs. Of family, and language, and truth. Awkward parts of it, life. But I won't go back. Not unless I've got something to write. This I finish. The trial will end. I hope that Darryl won't die. Not because he's good, but because he's alive. I wanted to drag every little thing I could think of this spring onto this platform with me, because birth is great and then it ends, the little head of the person is part of the world, with her weakness and her privilege, and the first grass of her life.

I HOPE THERE'S

MYSTERY

and

POETRY

IN YOUR LIFE

I woke up out of a dream the other night. I don't know what's going to happen to the class of 1998, but I'm happy to be alive with you. That's what I thought. I had this dream. I have to tell you about it. There was a caravan of beetles crossing the floor of the room I sleep in. They streamed over my dog's bowl, which was on the floor. And I started singing a song, not the words, just the music. It was the "Star Spangled Banner," and suddenly I was remembering late-night TV in the sixties, and we would see caravans of men on camels crossing a desert, and then jet planes would soar over a mosque, and we'd hear that song, and it was scary that before the TV went out in America, the station needed to say that we ruled the world. It gave my brother and me a chill. And then we went to bed. My dream just made me laugh and laugh, that beetles in my apartment could mean the same thing, and I wasn't alone. I told it to you, and she listened to me. I hope you all find yourselves sleeping with someone you love, maybe not all of the time, but a lot of the time. The touch of a foot in the night is sincere. I hope you like your work, I hope there's mystery and poetry in your life—not even poems, but patterns. I hope you can see them. Often these patterns will wake you up, and you will know that you are alive, again and again.

····· **EILEEN MYLES** ·····

is a widely recognized poet, essayist, and novelist who has published many works of poetry, fiction, plays, essays, articles, and libretti. Her recent works include *Snowflake/different streets*; *Inferno (A Poet's Novel)*, which is available on iTunes in her own voice; *The Importance of Being Iceland: Travel Essays in Art*; *Sorry, Tree*; and *Cool for You*. In 2012, she was awarded a Guggenheim Fellowship and in 2014 the Foundation for Contemporary Art awarded her a poetry fellowship. She lives in New York.

Jonathan Safran Foer

MIDDLEBURY COLLEGE, 2013

Note: The text below is Mr. Foer's abridgement of his talk into an OpEd piece in the *New York Times,* published on June 8, 2013. A video of the complete speech can be found online.

A couple of weeks ago, I saw a stranger crying in public. I was in Brooklyn's Fort Greene neighborhood, waiting to meet a friend for breakfast. I arrived at the restaurant a few minutes early and was sitting on the bench outside, scrolling through my contact list. A girl, maybe fifteen years old, was sitting on the bench opposite me, crying into her phone. I heard her say, "I know, I know, I know" over and over.

What did she know? Had she done something wrong? Was she being comforted? And then she said, "Mama, I know," and the tears came harder.

What was her mother telling her? Never to stay out all night again? That everybody fails? Is it possible that no one was on the other end of the call, and that the girl was merely rehearsing a difficult conversation?

"Mama, I know," she said, and hung up, placing her phone on her lap.

I was faced with a choice: I could interject myself into her life, or I could respect the boundaries between us. Intervening might make her feel worse, or be inappropriate. But then, it might ease her pain, or be helpful in some straightforward logistical way. An affluent neighborhood at the beginning of the day is not the same as a dangerous one as night is falling. And I was me, and not someone else. There was a lot of human computing to be done.

It is harder to intervene than not to, but it is vastly harder to choose to do either than to retreat into the scrolling names of one's contact list, or whatever one's favorite iDistraction happens to be. Technology celebrates connectedness, but encourages retreat. The phone didn't make me avoid the human connection, but it did make ignoring her easier in that moment, and more likely, by comfortably encouraging me to forget my choice to do so. My daily use of technological communication has been shaping me into someone more likely to forget others. The flow of water carves rock, a little bit at a time. And our personhood is carved, too, by the flow of our habits.

Psychologists who study empathy and compassion are finding that unlike our almost instantaneous responses to physical pain, it takes time for the brain to comprehend the psychological and moral dimensions of a situation. The more distracted we become, and the more emphasis we place on speed at the expense of depth, the less likely and able we are to care.

The

MORE DISTRACTED WE BECOME,

AND THE MORE
EMPHASIS WE PLACE ON

SPEED

AT THE EXPENSE OF

DEPTH,

THE LESS LIKELY
AND ABLE WE ARE TO

CARE.

WE ALL HAVE A SET
NUMBER OF DAYS TO
INDENT THE WORLD
WITH OUR *beliefs*, TO
FIND AND CREATE THE
beauty THAT ONLY
A FINITE EXISTENCE
ALLOWS FOR, TO WRESTLE
WITH THE QUESTION OF
purpose AND WRESTLE
WITH OUR *answers*.

Everyone wants his parent's, or friend's, or partner's undivided attention—even if many of us, especially children, are getting used to far less. Simone Weil wrote, "Attention is the rarest and purest form of generosity." By this definition, our relationships to the world, and to one another, and to ourselves, are becoming increasingly miserly.

Most of our communication technologies began as diminished substitutes for an impossible activity. We couldn't always see one another face to face, so the telephone made it possible to keep in touch at a distance. One is not always home, so the answering machine made a kind of interaction possible without the person being near his phone. Online communication originated as a substitute for telephonic communication, which was considered, for whatever reasons, too burdensome or inconvenient. And then texting, which facilitated yet faster, and more mobile, messaging. These inventions were not created to be improvements upon face-to-face communication, but a declension of acceptable, if diminished, substitutes for it.

But then a funny thing happened: We began to prefer the diminished substitutes. It's easier to make a phone call than to schlep to see someone in person. Leaving a message on someone's machine is easier than having a phone conversation—you can say what you need to say without a response; hard news is easier to leave; it's easier to check in without becoming entangled. So we began calling when we knew no one would pick up.

Shooting off an e-mail is easier still, because one can hide behind the absence of vocal inflection, and of course there's no chance of accidentally catching someone. And texting is even easier, as the expectation for articulateness is further reduced, and another shell is offered to hide in. Each step "forward" has made it easier, just a little, to avoid the emotional work of being present, to convey information rather than humanity.

The problem with accepting—with preferring—diminished substitutes is that over time, we, too, become diminished substitutes. People who become used to saying little become used to feeling little.

Being attentive to
the needs of others
might not be the
point of life, but it is
the work of life.

With each generation, it becomes harder to imagine a future that resembles the present. My grandparents hoped I would have a better life than they did: free of war and hunger, comfortably situated in a place that felt like home. But what futures would I dismiss out of hand for my grandchildren? That their clothes will be fabricated every morning on 3-D printers? That they will communicate without speaking or moving?

Only those with no imagination, and no grounding in reality, would deny the possibility that they will live forever. It's possible that many reading these words will never die. Let's assume, though, that we all have a set number of days to indent the world with our beliefs, to find and create the beauty that only a finite existence

People

USED TO SAYING

LITTLE

BECOME USED TO

FEELING

LITTLE.

allows for, to wrestle with the question of purpose and wrestle with our answers.

We often use technology to save time, but increasingly, it either takes the saved time along with it, or makes the saved time less present, intimate, and rich. I worry that the closer the world gets to our fingertips, the further it gets from our hearts. It's not an either/or—being "anti-technology" is perhaps the only thing more foolish than being unquestioningly "pro-technology"—but a question of balance that our lives hang upon.

Most of the time, most people are not crying in public, but everyone is always in need of something that another person can give, be it undivided attention, a kind word, or deep empathy. There is no better use of a life than to be attentive to such needs. There are as many ways to do this as there are kinds of loneliness, but all of them require attentiveness, all of them require the hard work of emotional computation and corporeal compassion. All of them require the human processing of the only animal who risks "getting it wrong" and whose dreams provide shelters and vaccines and words to crying strangers.

We live in a world made up more of story than stuff. We are creatures of memory more than reminders, of love more than likes. Being attentive to the needs of others might not be the point of life, but it is the work of life. It can be messy, and painful, and almost impossibly difficult. But it is not something we give. It is what we get in exchange for having to die.

····· **JONATHAN SAFRAN FOER** ·····

is the author of the award-winning and bestselling
novels *Everything Is Illuminated* and *Extremely Loud
and Incredibly Close* (both published by Houghton
Mifflin) as well as two works of nonfiction: *Eating
Animals* and *The New American Haggadah* (both
published by Little Brown). He was included in
Granta's "Best of Young American Novelists" issue
and in *The New Yorker*'s "20 under 40" list of the
best young writers in the U.S., and his books are
published in more than thirty languages.

Khaled Hosseini

VANDERBILT UNIVERSITY, 2010

On the eve of your graduation from Vanderbilt, one of the most distinguished houses of learning in this nation, I want to ask you a question about why we educate. Why do institutions go through the effort and money and all the energy to build colleges and universities to recruit the best and the brightest, and to teach them to the best of their ability? Why do you guys—the students—work years to get admitted, and you then scrounge around for funds so that you can attend the school, and then spend a fifth of your young lives in study?

You guys might say, well, because education is the key to greater opportunity, to prosperity. Education is where I get the skills I need, and I get a degree that stands as a mark of my experience and my knowledge. But what about the rest of us? What do we have at stake in this process? Why should we teach, why should we contribute to our alma maters? Why should we mentor young people coming out of college? And the answer is that the college and its graduates are part of our community. The people who learn today are going to work and exercise their ambitions tomorrow. We all have a vested interest in supporting the best thinkers and the best learners in our community.

You know, I remember my own education and the countless people who were there for me, who supported me, and who contributed to who I am today and what I have accomplished. So I recognize there is a debt that I owe. In other words, we have an appreciation for the process of learning.

And I want to talk for just a minute about what learning means—and that's something that you've all been doing for the last four years in this school. To me, learning is change. It's not an elaboration on a familiar set of knowledge. Learning occurs in those moments when we meet revelations. Learning is unexpected. Learning is a challenge to what you know or what you think you know—it's not a confirmation of it. Learning is a remapping of the world around you. And learning is not always comfortable, you know, it can alarm you. It can make you angry. But it will always make you think.

Here in school you've been lucky to have people to support you and to help you confront these moments and these challenges. But as you leave, bear in mind that you're not done yet, and that wherever you go, these challenges are going to seek you out, and they're going to find you. And the real test of your education here in Vanderbilt is how you're going to face these challenges on your own.

I'll give you the example of the burka, which is the full-body veil that has brought so much media attention to Afghanistan. In the West, the burka has become this familiar and iconic symbol of female oppression. A couple of years ago, a friend of mine came back from Afghanistan, where she'd gone to found a nonprofit to help Afghan women. She told me that before she went, she had these very strong visceral feelings about the burka, and it represented for her all that was wrong and all that was vexing about the situation of women in Afghanistan. It was, for her, a reliable barometer for social change in Afghanistan. And she felt that as things for women get better for women, people would shed the burka.

But she said that after she had lived there for a while, she came to see that all the media attention about the burka that it had received in the West was actually out of proportion with the reality that she found in Afghanistan. And she found that the burka was actually more important to her than it was to many women in Afghanistan. And she found that for many women she met, unveiling was actually not a primary preoccupation. They had other priorities. They were more worried about food, about shelter, about clean water, about education and healthcare, and many who wore the burka were actually very thoughtful, strong, decisive, and capable women. And so she came to see that just because a woman wore the veil didn't necessarily mean that she was not an active participant in her own future. And this was not easy for her to accept. It challenged her preconceived notions. But she left herself open to the challenge and open to a shift in the way that she perceived the world. And that's what learning is.

And that's going to happen to you. You're going to have these moments, whether you seek them out or not. And you won't be able to avoid them. You won't be able to avoid them because we live in a much smaller world today. Because of technology, we're far more connected than we were in the past to other people, other countries, other cultures. Even if you're the kind of person who's more comfortable in a small community. Even if you're the kind of person who avoids discussing political topics at a dinner table. Even if you read only those publications and those writers who share your opinions. New ideas and new points of view are going to find you. And you won't have a choice about that.

But what you do with these challenges is your choice. And that's not a question to take lightly. The easiest thing is to just ignore facts and feelings that don't match up with your idea of yourself and the world. We spend a lot of time, a lot of our life, building up our perception of people and events, and when something is out of step with that perception, it may seem like too much work to go back and rewrite everything. But in fact, that's what you've been practicing to do here in Vanderbilt for the last four years. And while leaving school may seem like the time to set your thoughts and your practices in stone, I would say that it's actually the time to experience and to experiment. And now that you're leaving these walls, I can think of no better way to honor your education and your learning than to use your skills to make this world a better place than the way you found it.

Because you get to determine the size of your world. It can be just you. Or, it could be your family, or your school. It could be your country. It could be your gender. It could be the people who share your opinions. Your world could be the people who share your interests, or people who share maybe a difficulty with you, maybe an illness. But it could be much more. And I will urge you, throughout your lives, to expand your knowledge by always expanding your community.

And a community is not just a bunch of people who have things in common. A community is a complicated organism, and it requires different people and different points of view in order to thrive. A complete community needs people who work with their hands, and people who work with their minds. It needs an older generation that's had years of experience, and it needs new blood to bring in innovation. It needs people who are cautious, and people who are bold. It needs women, and it needs men. It needs loyalists, and it needs critics.

NEW IDEAS AND NEW POINTS OF VIEW ARE GOING TO FIND YOU. AND YOU WON'T HAVE A CHOICE ABOUT THAT.

But very importantly, a community has to recognize, want, and care for its own. And sometimes, the people in a community who need the most help are the hardest to see—or, as the fable goes, those who cry out the least and suffer the most. So I'm going to ask something difficult of you. I'm going to ask that you seek out people in your community who are in need. And I'm going to ask you to try to not just understand them, but to help them. It's hard to make a connection with people who are suffering. It requires you to take on some of that pain for yourself. It makes you forge a kinship with misfortune, and to see how it could happen to you, and how it would make you feel.

There's an impulse to turn away from a beggar on the street. And we've all done that. Or from disturbing images on the TV screen. This impulse comes partly from this pain that we feel, absolutely. But, and this has to be said, I think it also comes from apathy, and apathy's insidious and enormously negative power. It was

EXPAND YOUR KNOWLEDGE BY ALWAYS EXPANDING YOUR COMMUNITY.

Helen Keller who said, "Science may have found a cure for most evils, but it has found no remedy for the worst of them all: the apathy of human beings."

Is this because we want to refute our connection to other people's problems? Have we, in this industrialized world, become lulled? Are we kind of like these tranquilized people who have no time to think of the hardship of people who are less fortunate than us? The great physician William Osler said that by far the most common foe we have to fight is apathy, indifference from whatever cause, not from a lack of knowledge but from carelessness, from absorption in other pursuits, from a contempt bred of self-satisfaction.

And it's easy to stage a dialogue in your mind, knowing that troubles exist and you're far away, but not knowing how you can help. And the argument goes something like this: I didn't do anything to contribute to this problem, so why should I feel responsible? Or you can say: I don't have the time or the money to fix this problem. And I think there's a real element of truth in this picture of how apathy comes to be. Or, maybe it has to do with not refuting the connection, but with the pain that we feel because we know that the connection is there, because we don't want to know that pain first hand and the easiest thing to do is to just not deal with it. Or, maybe apathy comes from the belief that we're helpless. That suffering is pervasive, and a way of life on this planet as long as there have been people on this planet. Poverty and the associated suffering are ubiquitous and inevitable in the human experience. Suffering in this world is so widespread and often of such mass scale that we feel defeated by it, and we slowly turn fatalistic and we lose our sense of moral urgency. Why try, when we can't change anything anyway?

But I would say that we need to be open to this pain. Because when we are, we have no choice but to help. It becomes our pain. And this is a difficult process, because it requires not just knowledge and not just learning, but very importantly, it requires imagination. And for that, for imagination, we need the tools to help us make that connection. To take something that is abstract and make it real. I know that in college all of you have taken courses that will prepare you for a specific career, and that's fine, but a full education requires humanities. It requires art. And the reason why those courses are given to you in this university is that art is a window into the minds of other people who are very different from you.

And I think in that regard the novel has a very unique ability. A couple of years ago, I read a book called *What Is the What* by Dave Eggers. It's a book about the trials of a South Sudanese refugee during Sudan's devastating civil war. What I knew about that war and had applied to the people of South Sudan had come from basically a random newspaper article. But after I read Dave Eggers's book, with its humanity and its humor and its compassion, that war came to me in a very real way every night when I sat down to read that book, and it made it impossible for me to gloss over the suffering of the people of South Sudan, because suddenly I felt like I knew who they were.

With regards to my own books, I get letters from India, from Tel Aviv, from Sydney, from London, and from Nashville. And people tell me that they want to send money to Afghanistan. One reader told me he wanted to adopt an Afghan orphan. And to me it's a great honor when readers write to me and say that Afghanistan for them is now more than just the caves of Tora Bora and the poppy fields of Helmand, and that they've come to see Afghanistan as more than just another chronically afflicted, troubled nation. In these letters I see the unique ability of art, especially the novel, to connect people

KNOW THE

MEASURE

of

YOUR OWN
POWERS.

through universal human experiences. So the arts are key in creating the understanding and compassion that drives you to help.

But what comes next? You have to have a practical course and some action that you can take. A mantra of the world of volunteer work and philanthropy is the idea of "give 5 percent." Give 5 percent of your time, or 5 percent of your money. It's a very small piece of your luck and your prosperity that you owe back to your community. It's something that all of us can manage. If you work forty hours per week, two hours spent with somebody less fortunate than you can make a world of difference.

I know this is a tall order, and it's a lot to ask of people who already have a lot on their plate. You have not inherited an easy world, and right now you might be wondering how you're going to face all of the changes that your life has in store for you. But I would say that to consider other people is not an additional burden, but rather an increased opportunity to be appreciated for who you are and what you're capable of. When you see the difference that you make in other people's world, you become alive to the changes that you can make in your own. And it's a way to be strong; it's a way to be wise, and to know the measure of your own powers.

You can also think of it as a chance to give the part of you that sparkles the brightest. If you're, say, a great writer or an avid reader, it's an opportunity to take your love and your skill and tutor in literacy. If you're good with your hands, maybe there's a house that needs building. If you're outgoing and you're charismatic, why not use that skill to make phone calls that connect with people and engage others in your cause.

Within the limits of my own set of skills, I have tried to do that on my own. I have tried to engage people around the world in my cause through the foundation, which was inspired by a 2007 trip

TWO HOURS

SPENT WITH SOMEBODY
LESS FORTUNATE THAN YOU

CAN MAKE A WORLD OF DIFFERENCE.

that I made to Afghanistan as a goodwill envoy for the United Nations Refugee Agency. I went to Northern Afghanistan and I met people who have come back to Afghanistan after ten, twenty years of living in Iran and Pakistan, fleeing the Taliban and the wars, and had come back to Afghanistan and they were living in the middle of nowhere, in a desert under tents or in cardboards, on less than a dollar per day, with no access to schools or healthcare or food, and they spent winters living in holes that they had dug in the ground. In the villages that I visited, the elders told me that they routinely lost ten to fifteen children every winter to the freezing temperatures. I'm a dad, and for me, as a dad, it was overwhelming and heartbreaking. As an Afghan, I felt connected to these people suffering, and I decided to do what I could to advocate for these people, and to give them a sense of control over their own lives, and to provide them with some basic services—especially shelter and education—so that they could get on with the business of rebuilding their broken country.

And in closing, for the rest of you, I wish you good fortune, and I wish you prosperity, and I wish you excitement in your new lives. I look forward to see what your generation is going to accomplish, with your great capacity to connect and to imagine. I know I have a lot to learn from you in the coming years, and I know that together we'll continue our education in the community of the world, where we can see ourselves in fellow human beings, be it in pain, or in passion, or in hope. And today I am honored to consider myself part of your community. Thank you so much.

····· KHALED HOSSEINI ·····

made his authorial debut with the novel *The Kite Runner*, which released to wide acclaim and has since sold in more than seventy countries. His subsequent novels, *A Thousand Splendid Suns* and *And the Mountains Echoed*, are *New York Times* bestsellers as well. He is also the founder of the Khaled Hosseini Foundation, a humanitarian nonprofit supporting the people of Afghanistan. Hosseini lives in northern California.

David Foster Wallace

KENYON COLLEGE, 2005

If anybody feels like perspiring [cough], I'd advise you to go ahead, because I'm sure going to. In fact I'm gonna [mumbles while pulling up his gown and taking out a handkerchief from his pocket].

Greetings, parents, and congratulations to Kenyon's graduating class of 2005. There are these two young fish swimming along and they happen to meet an older fish swimming the other way, who nods at them and says, "Morning, boys. How's the water?" And the two young fish swim on for a bit, and then eventually one of them looks over at the other and goes, "What the hell is water?"

This is a standard requirement of U.S. commencement speeches, the deployment of didactic little parable-ish stories. The story ["thing"] turns out to be one of the better, less bullshitty conventions of the genre, but if you're worried that I plan to present myself here as the wise, older fish explaining what water is to you younger fish, please don't be. I am not the wise old fish. The point of the fish story is merely that the most obvious, important realities are often the ones that are hardest to see and talk about. Stated as an English sentence, of course, this is just a banal platitude, but the fact is that in the day-to-day trenches of adult existence, banal platitudes can have a life-or-death importance, or so I wish to suggest to you on this dry and lovely morning.

THE MOST OBVIOUS, IMPORTANT REALITIES ARE OFTEN THE ONES THAT ARE HARDEST TO SEE AND TALK ABOUT.

Of course the main requirement of speeches like this is that I'm supposed to talk about your liberal arts education's meaning, to try to explain why the degree you are about to receive has actual human value instead of just a material payoff. So let's talk about the single most pervasive cliché in the commencement-speech genre, which is that a liberal arts education is not so much about filling you up with knowledge as it is about "teaching you how to think." If you're like me as a student, you've never liked hearing this, and you tend to feel a bit insulted by the claim that you needed anybody to teach you how to think, since the fact that you even got admitted to a college this good seems like proof that you already know how to think. But I'm going to posit to you that the liberal arts cliché turns out not to be insulting at all, because the really significant education in thinking that we're supposed to get in a place like this isn't really about the capacity to think, but rather about the choice of what to think about. If your total freedom of choice regarding what to think about seems too obvious to waste time discussing, I'd ask you to think about fish and water, and to bracket for just a few minutes your skepticism about the value of the totally obvious.

Here's another didactic little story. There are these two guys sitting together in a bar in the remote Alaskan wilderness. One of the guys is religious, the other is an atheist, and the two are arguing about the existence of God with that special intensity that comes after about the fourth beer. And the atheist says: "Look, it's not like I don't have actual reasons for not believing in God. It's not like I haven't ever experimented with the whole God and prayer thing. Just last month I got caught away from the camp in that terrible blizzard, and I was totally lost and I couldn't see a thing, and it was fifty below, and so I tried it: I fell to my knees in the snow and cried out 'Oh, God, if there is a God, I'm lost in this blizzard, and I'm gonna die if you don't help me.'" And now, in the bar, the religious guy looks at the atheist all puzzled. "Well then, you must believe now," he says. "After all, here you are, alive." The atheist just rolls his eyes. "No, man, all that was was a couple Eskimos happened to come wandering by and showed me the way back to camp."

It's easy to run this story through kind of a standard liberal arts analysis: The exact same experience can mean two totally different things to two different people, given those people's two different belief templates and two different ways of constructing meaning from experience. Because we prize tolerance and diversity of belief, nowhere in our liberal arts analysis do we want to claim that one guy's interpretation is true and the other guy's is false or bad.

Which is fine, except we also never end up talking about just where these individual templates and beliefs come from. Meaning, where they come from INSIDE the two guys. As if a person's most basic orientation toward the world and the meaning of his experience were somehow just hardwired, like height or shoe size, or automatically absorbed from the culture, like language. As if how we construct meaning were not actually a matter of personal, intentional choice. Plus, there's the whole matter of arrogance. The nonreligious guy is so totally certain in his dismissal of the possibility that the passing Eskimos had anything to do with his prayer for help. True, there are plenty of religious people who seem arrogant and certain of their own interpretations too. They're probably even more repulsive than atheists, at least to most of us. But religious dogmatists' problem is exactly the same as the story's unbeliever: blind certainty, a close-mindedness that amounts to an imprisonment so total that the prisoner doesn't even know he's locked up.

The point here is that I think this is one part of what "teaching me how to think" is really supposed to mean. To be just a little less arrogant. To have just a little critical awareness about myself and my certainties. Because a huge percentage of the stuff that I tend to be automatically certain of is, it turns out, totally wrong and deluded. I have learned this the hard way, as I predict you graduates will too.

Here is just one example of the total wrongness of something I tend to be automatically sure of: Everything in my own immediate experience supports my deep belief that I am the absolute center of the universe, the realest, most vivid and important person in existence. We rarely think about this sort of natural, basic self-centeredness because it's so socially repulsive. But it's pretty much the same for all of us. It is our default setting,

BE JUST A LITTLE LESS ARROGANT

hardwired into our boards at birth. Think about it: There is no experience you have had that you are not the absolute center of. The world as you experience it is there in front of YOU or behind YOU, to the left or right of YOU, on YOUR TV or YOUR monitor. And so on. Other people's thoughts and feelings have to be communicated to you somehow, but your own are so immediate, urgent, real.

Learning how to think really means learning how to exercise some control over how and what you think.

Please don't worry that I'm getting ready to lecture you about compassion or other-directedness or all the so-called virtues. This is not a matter of virtue. It's a matter of my choosing to do the work of somehow altering or getting free of my natural, hardwired default setting, which is to be deeply and literally self-centered and to see and interpret everything through this lens of self. People who can adjust their natural default setting this way are often described as being "well-adjusted," which I suggest to you is not an accidental term.

Given the triumphant academic setting here, an obvious question is how much of this work of adjusting our default setting involves actual knowledge or intellect. This question gets very tricky. Probably the most dangerous thing about an academic education—at least in my own case—is that it enables my tendency to over-intellectualize stuff, to get lost in abstract argument inside my head, instead of simply paying attention to what is going on right in front of me, paying attention to what is going on inside me.

As I'm sure you guys know by now, it is extremely difficult to stay alert and attentive, instead of getting hypnotized by the constant monologue inside your own head (may be happening right now). Twenty years after my own graduation, I have come gradually to understand that the liberal arts cliché about teaching you how to think is actually shorthand for a much deeper, more serious idea: Learning how to think really means learning how to exercise some control over how and what you think. It means being conscious and aware enough to choose what you pay attention to and to choose how you construct meaning from experience. Because if you cannot exercise this kind of choice in adult life, you will be totally hosed. Think of the old cliché about "the mind being an excellent servant but a terrible master."

This, like many clichés, so lame and unexciting on the surface, actually expresses a great and terrible truth. It is not the least bit coincidental that adults who commit suicide with firearms almost always shoot themselves in the head. They shoot the terrible master. And the truth is that most of these suicides are actually dead long before they pull the trigger.

And I submit that this is what the real, no bullshit value of your liberal arts education is supposed to be about: how to keep from going through your comfortable, prosperous, respectable adult life dead, unconscious, a slave to your head and to your natural default setting of being uniquely, completely, imperially alone day in and day out. That may sound like hyperbole, or abstract nonsense. Let's get concrete. The plain fact is that you graduating seniors do not yet have any clue what "day in day out" really means. There happen to be whole, large parts of adult American life that nobody talks about in commencement speeches. One such part involves boredom, routine, and petty frustration. The parents and older folks here will know all too well what I'm talking about.

By way of example, let's say it's an average adult day, and you get up in the morning, go to your challenging, white-collar, college-graduate job, and you work hard for eight or ten hours, and at the end of the day you're tired and somewhat stressed and all you want is to go home and have a good supper and maybe unwind for an hour, and then hit the sack early because, of course, you have to get up the next day and do it all again. But then you remember there's no food at home. You haven't had time to shop this week because of your challenging job, and so now after work you have to get in your car and drive to the supermarket. It's the end of the work day and the traffic is apt to be very bad. So getting to the store takes way longer than it should, and when you finally get there, the supermarket is very crowded, because of course it's the time of day when all the other people with jobs also try to squeeze in some grocery shopping. And the store is hideously lit and infused with soul-killing music or corporate pop, and it's pretty much the last place you want to be, but you can't just get in and quickly out; you have to wander all over the huge, over-lit store's confusing aisles to find the stuff you want and you have to maneuver your junky cart through all these other tired, hurried people with carts (et cetera, et cetera, cutting stuff out because this is a long ceremony) and eventually you get all your supper supplies, except now it turns out there aren't enough checkout lanes open even though it's the end-of-the-day rush. So the checkout line is incredibly long, which is stupid and infuriating. But you can't take your frustration out on the frantic lady working the register, who is overworked at a job whose daily tedium and meaninglessness surpasses the imagination of any of us here at a prestigious college.

But anyway, you finally get to the checkout line's front, and you pay for your food, and you get told to "Have a nice day" in a voice that is the absolute voice of death. Then you have to take your creepy, flimsy, plastic bags of groceries in your cart with the one crazy wheel that pulls maddeningly to the left, all the way out through the crowded, bumpy, littery parking lot, and then you have to drive all the way home through slow, heavy, SUV-intensive rush-hour traffic, et cetera, et cetera.

Everyone here has done this, of course. But it hasn't yet been part of you graduates' actual life routine, day after week after month after year.

But it will be. And many more dreary, annoying, seemingly meaningless routines besides. But that is not the point. The point is that petty, frustrating crap like this is exactly where the work of choosing is gonna come in. Because the traffic jams and crowded aisles and long checkout lines give me time to think, and if I don't make a conscious decision about how to think and what to pay attention to, I'm gonna be pissed and miserable every time I have to shop. Because my natural default setting is the certainty that situations like this are really all about me. About MY hungriness and MY fatigue and MY desire to just get home, and it's going to seem for all the world like everybody else is just in my way. And who are all these people in my way? And look at how repulsive most of them are, and how stupid and cow-like and dead-eyed and nonhuman they seem in the checkout line, or at how annoying and rude it is that people are talking loudly on cell phones in the middle of the line. And look at how deeply and personally unfair this is.

Or, of course, if I'm in a more socially conscious liberal arts form of my default setting, I can spend time in the end-of-the-day traffic being disgusted about all the huge, stupid, lane-blocking SUVs and Hummers and V-12 pickup trucks, burning their wasteful, selfish, forty-gallon tanks of gas, and I can dwell on the fact that the patriotic or religious bumper stickers always seem to be on the biggest, most disgustingly selfish vehicles, driven by the ugliest, [responding here to loud applause] (this is an example of how NOT to think, though) most disgustingly selfish vehicles, driven by the ugliest, most inconsiderate and aggressive drivers. And I can think about how our children's children will despise us for wasting all the future's fuel, and probably screwing up the climate, and how spoiled and stupid and selfish and disgusting we all are, and how modern consumer society just sucks, and so forth and so on.

You get the idea.

If I choose to think this way in a store and on the freeway, fine. Lots of us do. Except thinking this way tends to be so easy and automatic that it doesn't have to be a choice. It is my natural default setting. It's the automatic way that I experience the boring, frustrating, crowded parts of adult life when I'm operating on the automatic, unconscious belief that I am the center of the world and that my immediate needs and feelings are what should determine the world's priorities.

The thing is that, of course, there are totally different ways to think about these kinds of situations. In this traffic, all these vehicles stopped and idling in my way, it's not impossible that some of these people in SUVs have been in horrible auto accidents in the past, and now find driving so terrifying that their therapist has all but ordered them to get a huge, heavy SUV so they can feel safe enough to drive. Or that the Hummer that just cut me off is maybe being driven by a father whose little child is hurt or sick in the seat next to him, and he's trying to get this kid to the hospital, and he's in a bigger, more legitimate hurry than I am: It is actually I who am in HIS way.

IT TAKES WILL AND EFFORT, AND IF YOU ARE LIKE ME, SOME DAYS YOU WON'T BE ABLE TO DO IT, OR YOU JUST FLAT OUT WON'T WANT TO.

Or I can choose to force myself to consider the likelihood that everyone else in the supermarket's checkout line is just as bored and frustrated as I am, and that some of these people probably have harder, more tedious and painful lives than I do.

Again, please don't think that I'm giving you moral advice, or that I'm saying you are supposed to think this way, or that anyone expects you to just automatically do it. Because it's hard. It takes will and effort, and if you are like me, some days you won't be able to do it, or you just flat out won't want to.

But most days, if you're aware enough to give yourself a choice, you can choose to look differently at this fat, dead-eyed, over-made-up lady who just screamed at her kid in the checkout line. Maybe she's not usually like this. Maybe she's been up three straight nights holding the hand of a husband who is dying of bone cancer. Or maybe this very lady is the low-wage clerk at the motor vehicle department, who just yesterday helped your spouse resolve a horrific, infuriating red-tape problem through some small act of bureaucratic kindness. Of course, none of this is likely, but it's also not impossible. It just depends what you want to consider. If you're automatically sure that you know what reality is, and you are operating on your default setting, then you, like me, probably won't consider possibilities that aren't annoying and miserable. But if you really learn how to pay attention, then you will know there are other options. It will actually be within your power to experience a crowded, hot, slow, consumer-hell type situation as not only meaningful, but sacred, on fire with the same force that made the stars: love, fellowship, the mystical oneness of all things deep down.

Not that that mystical stuff is necessarily true. The only thing that's capital-T True is that you get to decide how you're gonna try to see it.

This, I submit, is the freedom of a real education, of learning how to be well-adjusted. You get to consciously decide what has meaning and what doesn't. You get to decide what to worship.

Because here's something else that's weird but true: In the day-to-day trenches of adult life, there is actually no such thing as atheism. There is no such thing as not worshipping. Everybody worships. The only choice we get is what to worship. And the compelling reason for maybe choosing some sort of god or spiritual-type thing to worship—be it JC or Allah, be it YHWH, or the Wiccan Mother Goddess, or the Four Noble Truths, or some inviolable set of ethical principles—is that pretty much anything else you worship will eat you alive. If you worship money and things, if they are where you tap real meaning in life, then you will never have

YOU GET TO CONSCIOUSLY

DECIDE
WHAT HAS
MEANING

AND WHAT DOESN'T.

The
REALLY
IMPORTANT
KIND OF FREEDOM
INVOLVES
ATTENTION
AND AWARENESS
AND DISCIPLINE,

AND BEING ABLE TRULY TO CARE ABOUT
OTHER PEOPLE AND TO SACRIFICE FOR
THEM OVER AND OVER IN MYRIAD PETTY,

UNSEXY WAYS
EVERY DAY.

enough, never feel you have enough. It's the truth. Worship your body and beauty and sexual allure and you will always feel ugly. And when time and age start showing, you will die a million deaths before they finally grieve you. On one level, we all know this stuff already. It's been codified as myths, proverbs, clichés, epigrams, parables: the skeleton of every great story. The whole trick is keeping the truth up front in daily consciousness.

Worship power, you will end up feeling weak and afraid, and you will need ever more power over others to numb you to your own fear. Worship your intellect, being seen as smart, you will end up feeling stupid, a fraud, always on the verge of being found out. But the insidious thing about these forms of worship is not that they're evil or sinful, it's that they're unconscious. They are default settings.

They're the kind of worship you just gradually slip into, day after day, getting more and more selective about what you see and how you measure value without ever being fully aware that that's what you're doing.

And the so-called real world will not discourage you from operating on your default settings, because the so-called real world of men and money and power hums merrily along in a pool of fear and anger and frustration and craving and worship of self. Our own present culture has harnessed these forces in ways that have yielded extraordinary wealth and comfort and personal freedom. The freedom for all to be lords of our tiny, skull-sized kingdoms, alone at the center of all creation. This kind of freedom has much to recommend it. But of course there are all different kinds of freedom, and the kind that is most precious you will not hear much talk about in the great outside world of wanting and achieving . . . The really important kind of freedom involves attention and awareness and discipline, and being able truly to care about other people and to sacrifice for them over and over in myriad petty, unsexy ways every day.

That is real freedom. That is being educated, and understanding how to think. The alternative is unconsciousness, the default setting, the rat race, the constant gnawing sense of having had, and lost, some infinite thing.

I know that this stuff probably doesn't sound fun and breezy or grandly inspirational the way a commencement speech is supposed to sound. What it is, as far as I can see, is the capital-T Truth, with a whole lot of rhetorical niceties stripped away. You are, of course, free to think of it whatever you wish. But please don't just dismiss it as just some finger-wagging Dr. Laura sermon. None of this stuff is really about morality or religion or dogma or big fancy questions of life after death.

The capital-T Truth is about life BEFORE death.

It is about the real value of a real education, which has almost nothing to do with knowledge, and everything to do with simple awareness: awareness of what is so real and essential, so hidden in plain sight all around us, all the time, that we have to keep reminding ourselves over and over:

"This is water."

"This is water."

It is unimaginably hard to do this, to stay conscious and alive in the adult world day in and day out. Which means yet another grand cliché turns out to be true: your education really IS the job of a lifetime. And it commences: now.

I wish you way more than luck.

····· DAVID FOSTER WALLACE ·····

(1962–2008) was an American author whose
best-known works include acclaimed novels *Infinite
Jest*, *The Broom of the System*, and Pulitzer
Prize–finalist *The Pale King*, as well as the short
story collections *Oblivion* and *Brief Interviews with
Hideous Men*. Wallace also published articles in
Rolling Stone, *Harper's Magazine*, the *New Yorker*,
and many other international periodicals. Among his
many honors are a MacArthur Fellowship and
a Whiting Writer's award.

CREDITS

This book was made possible thanks to generous contributions by the following: